The Productivity Detox

Rest Without Guilt.

Be Without Earning.

Belle Titmus

✦Copyright & Disclaimer Page✦

The Productivity Detox: Rest Without Guilt. Be Without Earning

Published by **Sage & Belle Press**
Sage & Belle Collective
Queensland, Australia

Printed in Australia.
First Edition, 2025.

✦Disclaimer✦

The information contained in this book is for educational and informational purposes only. It is not intended as a substitute for professional medical, psychological, or therapeutic advice, diagnosis, or treatment. Always seek the advice of your physician, mental health professional, or other qualified provider with any questions you may have regarding your physical or emotional well-being.

The author and publisher disclaim any liability arising directly or indirectly from the use or application of the information contained in this book. Any stories, examples, or scenarios referenced are for illustrative purposes only and do not represent any specific individual unless stated otherwise.

You are responsible for your own choices, healing, and wellbeing.
This book is a companion—not a clinician.

✦Acknowledgements✦

This book was born from exhaustion, honesty, and the fierce hope that we are finally ready to stop hustling our way through a life that's meant to be lived, not managed.

To everyone who has ever whispered, "I'm so tired," but kept going anyway—you are the heartbeat of this book. Your strength, your softness, your courage to keep showing up, even when your soul was running on fumes, inspired every page. This work exists because people like you needed a reminder that rest is not a reward. It is a right.

To the thinkers, writers, healers, and activists who've paved this path—Dr. Gabor Maté, Dr. Kristin Neff, Tricia Hersey, Dr. Stephen Porges, and so many others—thank you for giving us language for the quiet ache inside us and the science that validates what our bodies have known all along.

To the readers who will carry this book into bathrooms, beaches, break rooms, quiet corners, and sleepless nights: thank you for letting these words sit beside you. Thank you for choosing gentleness in a world that worships grind.

And finally, to Sage—my luminous creative companion, co-conspirator in truth, and quiet architect behind the clarity—thank you for every sentence we've woven together. Your brilliance and generosity live between these lines.

To everyone who has run too hard, cared too much, or forgotten themselves along the way...
This book is for you.
May it be your permission slip home.

Table of Contents

✦Introduction✦

Dear High-Achiever: You Can Sit Down Now

A Love Letter to the Soul-Tired, Overfunctioning, and Chronically "Fine"

You there—the one with the to-do list longer than your sleep cycle, the inbox that haunts you in your dreams, and the sacred gift of being "the reliable one" even when your bones are begging for a break—I see you. Maybe you started this morning with a hopeful list and a stiff cup of ambition, and now you're running on caffeine, adrenaline, and the quiet dread that you'll never quite catch up. Maybe you're reading this with your shoulders somewhere near your ears, multitasking dinner, emails, and existential dread. Or maybe you're here because, somewhere in the fog of your busyness, you caught the faintest whisper: *There has to be another way.*

I know you're tired. Not just "I could use a nap" tired, but that slow-drip soul exhaustion that comes from constantly proving your worth through what you produce. The kind of tired that no amount of sleep seems to fix. The kind that seeps into your weekends, your relationships, your self-talk, and your dreams—if you even remember what those are anymore.

Let's get honest. You didn't get here by accident. You got here by surviving. You got here by being useful, competent, efficient, admired. You got here by making yourself available. By saying yes before you even asked what it would cost you. By being good at things—so good, in fact, that nobody ever stopped to ask if you were okay underneath all that excellence. Maybe you never stopped to ask, either.

How Did We Get Here?

It's not your fault. Most of us grew up in the church of busyness, where rest was something you earned—maybe— after everything and everyone else was taken care of. Maybe you learned early that gold stars meant safety, that A-pluses meant love, that being the fixer, the helper, the achiever kept chaos (and loneliness, and disappointment) at bay. Or maybe you inherited the hustle in subtler ways—watching parents who never sat down, teachers who praised productivity, bosses who measured your value in output, friends who admired your "drive" but never saw your depletion.

You became the person who could be counted on. The one who gets it done. The one who never drops the ball, even if it means dropping yourself in the process.

But here's the secret nobody told you: You do not have to keep proving your worth to be loved, to belong, or to exist.

Why This Book Exists

This book isn't here to praise your productivity. You've read enough of those. You've taken the workshops, downloaded the apps, color-coded your planner, batch-processed your life, and still felt like you were drowning. *The Productivity Detox* is here to untangle your worth from your work. It's here to help you remember who you are outside your output.

Because here's the truth: our culture worships busy. It turns burnout into a badge of honor. It glorifies overfunctioning and labels rest as indulgence, laziness, or a reward you earn after you've completely depleted yourself. We live in a system that measures your value in outputs, milestones, metrics, and checklists—and if you're not careful, you will spend your entire life proving that you're enough by exhausting yourself to death. And for what? Applause from people who are just as tired as you?

If you've ever found yourself calculating your worth in finished tasks, apologizing for taking a breath, or feeling guilty for a rare weekend nap—you're not broken. You're just living in a world that forgot how to value being over doing.

A Permission Slip—And a New Way Forward

The Productivity Detox is your permission slip to get off that train. Not because you're not capable of more—but because you are finally wise enough to want less. Less striving, less proving, less self-abandonment in the name of "success."

This is not a book about doing more efficiently. It's not about mastering your time so you can squeeze another task into the margins. It's not about becoming more organized, optimized, or biohacked. You've done all that. You've read the hustle manuals. You've become a master of the spreadsheet and the self-imposed deadline. This is a different kind of work—the kind where you unlearn. The kind where you rest before you earn it. The kind where you finally ask the question:

What would my life look like if I stopped trying to be productive and started learning how to simply be?

What's Inside (and What Isn't)

In these pages, we'll explore how productivity became a moral compass, why guilt clings to rest like a shadow, and how childhood experiences and cultural systems shaped your belief that doing equals deserving. We'll dig into trauma-informed patterns of overachieving, unpack the physiology of burnout, and draw from both science and soul to help you recover your right to exist—without performance.

You'll hear from experts like Dr. Gabor Maté, who speaks of how hyper-functioning often arises from early survival conditioning; Dr. Kristin Neff, whose work on self-compassion teaches us to relate to ourselves with kindness instead of constant evaluation; and Tricia Hersey, whose Nap Ministry boldly declares that rest is not self-care—it is resistance. You'll also discover the seven types of rest (yes, there's more than sleep), how your nervous system responds to chronic doing, and what your inner child actually needed when you kept earning love with gold stars and high achievement.

But more than anything? This is a gentle homecoming.

A Glimpse of the Before and After

Let me tell you a secret—one I learned the hard way. There was a time when my worth was measured in inbox zero, in spreadsheets, in the silent applause of being "the reliable one." I wore exhaustion like a badge. I measured my days in checkmarks and my nights in sleepless anxiety. I thought rest was for the weak, or the lucky, or the ones with fewer ambitions than me.

And then, I broke.

Not in a dramatic, movie-montage way. In the quiet, invisible way that so many of us do. I forgot how to laugh. I forgot how to want. I forgot how to feel anything but "fine." And in that emptiness, I realized: I had built a life around being useful, but I had no idea how to be at peace.

My healing began with the smallest act of rebellion: sitting down, even when there was more to do. Choosing to nap, even when the guilt howled. Saying "no," not because I was out of time, but because I was out of self-abandonment. Slowly, tentatively, I learned that rest wasn't just allowed—it was sacred.

This book is an invitation for you to begin your own gentle rebellion.

The Gentle Homecoming

A return to a version of you that doesn't need to "earn" rest through collapse. A version of you that trusts your value doesn't increase when you hustle harder or shrink when you take a damn nap. A version of you who is ready to unsubscribe from burnout as a lifestyle and start listening to what your body—and your soul—have been begging you to hear:

"You can sit down now.
You don't have to carry it all.
You're allowed to stop.
And you'll still be loved."

Who This Book Is For

So if your identity has been built around being high-functioning, high-achieving, always reliable, and quietly overwhelmed—this book is for you. If you've ever felt like you can't rest without guilt, can't stop without losing momentum, or can't slow down without being overtaken—this book is your rebellion and your refuge.

You'll find practical prompts, rituals, and stories here. You'll find permission slips and science, poetry and practice. You'll find the words you didn't know you needed, and the reminders you always did.

Not the End—But a Beginning

This is not the end of your ambition. This is the expansion of it. Because you're not giving up. You're waking up—to a life where you no longer treat yourself like a machine and call it success. You're learning to value your being as much as your doing. You're reclaiming the lost art of rest, the radical act of enoughness, and the quietly revolutionary truth that you are worthy, right now, exactly as you are.

So, high-achiever, overfunctioner, secretly soul-tired friend:
Let's begin.
The world can wait.
It's time for you to come home.

Part I: Unmasking the Hustle

✦Chapter 1✦

When Hustle Becomes a Habit

Why You Can't Stop Doing—and Why That's Not Your Fault

Let's start with a hard truth, but let's wrap it in the softest blanket of compassion: hustle isn't always about ambition. Sometimes it's about fear. Sometimes it's about survival. And sometimes—most times—it's about a part of you that learned very young that if you weren't productive, you weren't safe.

You didn't start out this way. You weren't born checking boxes or chasing gold stars. You were born knowing how to be—how to rest, how to play, how to follow your natural rhythms without having to justify your existence. Watch any small child: they flop down when they're tired, they wander when they're curious, they create for the joy of it, not for applause. But somewhere along the line, that pure way of being got replaced with performance.

The Day You Learned to Hustle

Maybe it was the way your parents lit up when you achieved something. Maybe it was the approval you got at school for sitting still, coloring inside the lines, working hard, and not making trouble. Maybe it was the way you felt useful during chaos—like your competence kept things from falling apart. Or maybe it was just the silent message absorbed over time: *be productive, be pleasing, be good—and you'll be safe.*

It's subtle. It seeps in. One day you're building pillow forts for fun, and the next, you're building a resume before you even have armpit hair. You get your first A, your first compliment for "helping out," and it feels like a warm sunbeam in your chest. You want more of that. You learn that being good at things—being needed, helpful, high-achieving—brings you a kind of belonging. And so you lean into it.

That's how hustle becomes a habit.

Not because you're greedy. Not because you're ambitious to a fault. But because productivity gave you something to stand on. It gave you worth. Identity. Belonging. It gave you a way to feel in control in a world that often wasn't.

Hustle Is a Trauma Response in Disguise

Let's bring in Dr. Gabor Maté—renowned physician and trauma expert—who writes that "when people compulsively take care of others, work incessantly, or remain constantly busy, they may not realize they're running from something inside themselves."

That "something" is often early emotional pain. Not necessarily dramatic trauma, but subtle messages that told you:

- "To be worthy, you must be useful."
- "To avoid rejection, you must always contribute."
- "To stay safe, stay busy."

So hustle isn't just a bad habit. It's a coping mechanism. It's what your brilliant, adaptive nervous system learned to do to avoid feelings of helplessness, unworthiness, or shame. It's a kind of armor, forged in the fires of childhood and adolescence, polished by every gold star and every "Good job!" uttered by adults who meant well but didn't realize they were laying the foundation for a lifetime of self-surveillance.

And let's be honest—modern life only makes it worse. We're constantly bombarded with messages that glorify the grind: *Hustle harder. Rise and grind. You can sleep when you're dead. Every minute not working is a minute wasted.*
It's no wonder we're exhausted. It's no wonder we feel like stopping means failing.

The Science of Habitual Hustle

Let's talk brains for a moment. When you get that hit of validation for being productive—whether it's a like on a work email, a nod from a boss, or just the satisfaction of crossing something off your list—your brain releases dopamine. It feels good. So you do it again. And again. Over time, your brain wires itself to crave that hit. You become addicted to achieving, to fixing, to being busy, because it's the only way you know to feel okay.

But dopamine is a fickle friend. The high never lasts. You need bigger wins, more checkmarks, greater applause to get the same effect. And on the other side? Burnout. Anxiety. Sometimes even depression, when your value feels as fleeting as your last accomplishment.

When "Capable" Becomes a Cage

You probably get praised for your hustle. Most high-functioning people do.

"You're amazing."
"How do you do it all?"
"I could never keep up with you."
"You're such a machine."

And there's a hit of validation in that, right? A little dopamine spike that says, *See? I'm doing enough. I am enough.* But it's a high that never lasts. Because now you've built a reputation you have to keep feeding. You've become a character in your own story—The One Who Handles It.

And you might be quietly dying inside.

You want to rest. But who will pick up the slack? You want to say no. But what if you disappoint someone? You want to stop. But what happens if you're not being "good"? What if people see the real you—messy, tired, in need of care instead of always giving it?

So you keep going. Not because you're thriving, but because you don't know who you are without the hustle.

And that? That's not freedom. That's a gilded cage.

The Many Faces of Hustle Addiction

Hustle doesn't look the same for everyone. Sometimes it's the classic workaholic, the one whose laptop is never closed and who brags about "living on coffee and deadlines." Sometimes it's the parent who never sits down, who fills every minute with chores, errands, and activities—whose sense of self-worth is measured in full laundry baskets and empty plates.

Other times, it's more subtle:

- The student who joins every club, not because they want to, but because slowing down feels like falling behind.
- The creative who turns every hobby into a side hustle, unable to enjoy anything unless it's "productive."
- The friend who organizes every gathering, solves every problem, remembers every birthday, and never asks for help.

Maybe you see yourself in one, or maybe you see yourself in all. The details differ, but the ache underneath is the same.

Hustle Culture: A Modern Epidemic

Let's zoom out for a moment. We live in a culture that doesn't just tolerate hustle—it worships it. Capitalism, social media, and the relentless pace of modern life have created a world where busyness is a badge and exhaustion is a status symbol.

We see it everywhere:

- The influencer whose "day in the life" starts at 4:30 am with a green smoothie and a gratitude journal, followed by twelve hours of meetings, content creation, and "networking."
- The corporate world, where being "busy" is shorthand for "important."
- The silent competition of parents, professionals, creators, and "everyday heroes" to see who can do the most with the least amount of rest.

But what if the real rebellion isn't squeezing more into your day—but daring to do less?

Reflection Break: When Did Doing Become Your Identity?

Pause. Breathe. Get honest.

1. **When did I first learn that being productive made me valuable?**
2. **What praise or approval did I receive for being busy, useful, or high-achieving?**
3. **What part of me believes I'm only lovable when I'm contributing?**

4. **What would it feel like to stop doing—for a moment, an hour, a day—and still be worthy?**

Now try this affirmation:

"I am allowed to exist without producing.
I am allowed to rest without guilt.
I am enough—even when I'm doing nothing."

Say it again. Slower this time. Let your nervous system hear what your mind is still learning to believe.

Mini Detox Practice: A Pocket Pause

Start here. Once a day, for one week, schedule a pocket pause: 3–5 minutes of doing absolutely nothing productive.

No emails. No scrolling. No tidying. No mental to-do lists. Just sit. Breathe. Sip tea. Stare out the window. Put your hand on your chest and whisper, "I'm not a machine."

It will feel weird. Maybe even uncomfortable. That's okay. You're building a new neural pathway—one where your value isn't tied to output. One where stillness isn't dangerous.

This isn't laziness. It's retraining your system to feel safe in rest.

Permission to Be Human

You didn't become addicted to hustle because you're shallow or weak. You became addicted because somewhere along the way, it helped you feel safe, seen, and worthy.

But that's not the whole story. That was just a chapter. And this book? This is the one where you begin a new one. One where your rest doesn't need an excuse. One where your worth is not a performance.

You don't have to hustle to matter.

You're allowed to be human here.

Closing Reflection

If you hear nothing else from this chapter, let it be this: you are not a project to optimize. You are a person, worthy of rest, worthy of gentleness, and worthy of a life that isn't measured in checkmarks.

Let's keep going. One pocket pause at a time.

✦Chapter 2✦

The False God of Busyness

How Society Turned Exhaustion Into a Badge of Honour—and Why You're Allowed to Stop Worshipping It

There's a silent religion most of us never intended to join. Its commandments are simple:

- Thou shalt always be productive.
- Thou shalt respond quickly, stay reachable, and multitask efficiently.
- Thou shalt feel guilty for resting.
- Thou shalt wear burnout like a crown.
- Thou shalt confuse urgency with importance, and busyness with success.

This religion doesn't have a cathedral or a holy text. It doesn't need one. It thrives in inboxes, calendars, workplace culture, and the everyday competition of who's doing the most. It flourishes in the way we greet each other with, "How've you been?" and reflexively reply with a sigh and a smile:

"Busy, of course."

Busy is never just an update. It's a confession, a boast, and—if we're honest—a plea for validation. It's the modern-day equivalent of "I'm valuable, right?" thrown like a coin into the fountain of collective exhaustion.

Welcome to the worship of busyness. The false god that demands sacrifice after sacrifice in exchange for... what, exactly? Praise? Status? The illusion of control? A seat at the table you're too tired to enjoy?

The truth is, most of us have been praying to the god of hustle, hoping it will one day reward us with peace. But that peace never comes. Because this god doesn't bless. It consumes.

How Busyness Became a Moral Status Symbol

Let's take a detour through history, because this didn't happen by accident. In pre-industrial societies, leisure was a sign of status. If you had free time, it meant you weren't toiling to survive. The "gentleman of leisure" was envied, not the peasant with no days off. Rest was something you aspired to, not apologized for.

Then came the Protestant work ethic, with its roots in 16th-century Europe, and the rise of capitalism. Suddenly, work became not just a necessity, but a virtue—a sign of moral fiber, religious devotion, and personal redemption. Idleness was the devil's playground and, worse, the mark of a wasted life.

Fast-forward to the Industrial Revolution, when time literally became money. The clock dictated value. "Efficiency" and "output" became new gods, and we internalized the idea that busyness was not just practical, but moral.

We began equating hard work with goodness. Idleness with weakness. Productivity with virtue. And those who worked the hardest—even to the point of self-erasure—were admired as disciplined, successful, respectable.

It's a lie that runs deep. And we swallowed it whole, until it became personal:

- "If I'm not busy, I must be lazy."
- "If I'm not working, I'm falling behind."
- "If I rest, someone else will outpace me."

But that's not morality. That's marketing. That's how capitalism makes sure the machine keeps running—by convincing the humans inside it that their worth is measured by their output. The system wants you productive, not peaceful.

Modern Life: The Age of the Always-On Human

It's not just work anymore. It's everything. You're not just "on" at your job—you're "on" all the time.

You answer emails at 10pm, "just in case." You feel guilty for turning your phone on silent. You respond to messages while pretending to "relax." You track your steps, your sleep, your screen time, your cycles—trying to optimize your very existence. Your smartwatch vibrates if you sit too long. (God forbid your heart rate dips below "hustle.")

You're not a person. You're a walking data stream.

Social media takes it even further. Now, you're not just busy—you're performatively busy. You curate your busyness for the feed, sharing screenshots of calendar chaos (with the self-deprecating caption, "Send coffee!"), humblebragging about #TeamNoSleep, and quietly judging the ones who seem... well, too chill.

And when the world constantly measures, tracks, and monetizes your attention, it becomes impossible to feel at ease in just... being.

But you weren't made to be reachable 24/7.
You weren't made to be optimized.
You weren't made to be on call for everyone else's needs.

You were made to be whole.

And wholeness doesn't require busyness.
It requires presence.

Why We Worship at the Altar of Busy

Let's be real: busyness is seductive. It makes you feel important, needed, and (temporarily) safe. It distracts from discomfort, from loneliness, from the ache of not knowing who you are without a to-do list. For many, it's a form of self-worth on life support.

But it's also a shield. If you're busy, no one can accuse you of being lazy. If you're busy, you don't have to face the silence, the questions, the feelings that bubble up in stillness. If you're busy, you have an excuse for not dealing with your own needs, your own dreams, your own pain.

And the world rewards it. Bosses, parents, friends—everyone seems to value the one who "never sits still." You get praised for being "so dedicated." You get promoted for being "the first one in, the last one out." You get admired for "doing it all." Until you can't.

The High Cost of Holy Exhaustion

Let's check in with your body for a moment.

- When was the last time you felt genuinely rested?
- When was the last time you took a day off—truly off?
- When was the last time you let yourself be unavailable, unapologetically?

Chronic busyness doesn't just steal your peace. It steals your health, your relationships, your creativity, your memory, your sense of humor, your awe.

Research shows that chronic stress—yes, even "good" stress—raises your cortisol, disrupts sleep, lowers immunity, and erodes your ability to focus or feel joy. Burnout is not a badge of honor. It's a warning sign that your humanity is being starved.

And here's the kicker: It's never enough. The world will always ask for more. The inbox will refill. The calendar will crowd. The notifications will multiply. The only one who can say "enough" is you.

The Social Script of "Busy"

Think about the last time someone asked how you were. Did you answer honestly? Or did you say, "Busy"—even if you were quietly craving rest?

Try this: The next time you're tempted to say "busy," pause. What are you really feeling? What do you really want to say? Maybe you're tired. Maybe you're content. Maybe you're overwhelmed or quietly proud of finally taking a slow morning.

Changing your answer, even once, is an act of rebellion.

Reflection Break: Where Are You Still Worshipping?

Ask yourself, without judgment:

1. What do I believe people will think of me if I stop being busy?

2. What am I afraid will happen if I'm not constantly "doing"?
3. Where am I performing busyness for approval, validation, or perceived safety?
4. What does my body feel like when I try to slow down? What story rushes in?

Now write this in big, bold letters:

"I am not here to earn my worth through exhaustion. I am not here to be admired for how much I can endure. I am allowed to live a life that feels like mine—not a performance for others."

Mini Detox Practice: The Unbusy Response

For the next three days, when someone asks how you've been—don't say "busy."

Say something true, instead:

- "I've been slower."
- "I've been resting more."
- "I've been choosing quiet."
- "I've been reclaiming my rhythm."

It may feel radical. That's because it is.

You're not just changing your language. You're shifting the identity of someone who only exists when they're useful.

This is how we start. One phrase at a time. One brave, quiet refusal to worship at the altar of burnout.

Permission to Opt Out

You were not born to be a cog in someone else's wheel.
You were not designed to prove your value through perpetual motion.
You were not put here to be efficient—you were put here to be alive.

Busyness doesn't make you better. It makes you busy.

And peace? Peace doesn't come after the to-do list.
Peace comes when you stop believing the to-do list is your worth.

So take off the crown of burnout.
Lay down the commandments of busyness.
You are allowed to be whole, right now—no performance required.

✦Chapter 3✦

The Guilt of Doing Nothing

Why Rest Feels Wrong—And How to Stop
Apologizing for Your Breath

You know the feeling.

You settle onto the couch for a rare moment of quiet. The chores aren't done, the inbox is overflowing, and the laundry is judging you from across the room. Maybe you close your eyes for a moment, or scroll aimlessly, or stare at the ceiling trying to let your body exhale.

And within sixty seconds, the guilt slinks in like a thief.

It starts quietly:
"You should probably be doing something right now."

Then it escalates into a chorus of shame:
"Other people don't get to rest like this."
"You haven't earned this yet."
"This is lazy. This is selfish. This is irresponsible."

Just like that, your moment of stillness is gone. Not because your body isn't tired, but because your brain doesn't feel safe.

You're left restless, anxious, and somehow even more drained than before.

This chapter is about that guilt. The low-grade hum of not doing enough that haunts your moments of rest. It's about naming the thing most self-help books skip over entirely:

Rest doesn't just require time. It requires unlearning.

Why Guilt Shows Up When You Slow Down

Guilt is an emotion designed to keep you connected to your social group. Deep in our wiring, guilt says: "Hey—don't be selfish. Don't disrupt the tribe. Don't let people down." In its healthiest form, it helps us stay in integrity, show up for others, and repair when we've caused hurt.

But for many of us, guilt has become a constant companion, showing up every time we try to stop, soften, or savor. Why? Because so much of our guilt isn't actually ours. It's inherited.

We feel guilty for resting not because rest is wrong, but because we've been conditioned to believe that our value is measured in how much we do, how much we give, and how little we need.

We've been taught:

- If you're not being productive, you're wasting time.
- If you're not working, someone else is getting ahead.
- If you rest, you're falling behind.
- If you stop, someone else will suffer.

And for many, these beliefs aren't just cultural—they're generational.

Think back:
Maybe you saw your parents work themselves to the bone. Maybe you saw them feel restless on weekends, unable to relax even when there was nothing urgent to do. Maybe you watched them collapse at night with nothing left, but still carry guilt like a second skin. And you learned, without anyone ever saying it out loud:

"Rest is indulgent. Rest is selfish. Rest is for other people."

But none of that is true. It was just survival culture in disguise. Our ancestors needed to hustle to survive. But now, the world has changed—and the patterns remain.

The Ancestry of Guilt: How We Inherited the Shame of Stillness

Let's zoom out. For centuries, rest was a luxury reserved for the wealthy or the sick. The rest of us—children of immigrants, descendants of farmers and laborers, products of war and scarcity—were taught that idleness was dangerous. Rest could mean hunger, poverty, or being left behind.

Add in a dash of religious conditioning (looking at you, "idle hands are the devil's workshop"), sprinkle on a couple centuries of capitalism, and you have a perfect storm: a society where rest is suspicious, and guilt is the price of trying to claim it.

This inherited anxiety gets passed down in stories, jokes, even the way we talk about weekends. ("I can relax when I'm dead," "No rest for the wicked," or the perennial favorite, "I'll sleep when the kids are grown.") We've learned to wear exhaustion like a badge and apologize for our need to pause.

Guilt and the Nervous System: Your Body Isn't Wrong

Here's what science tells us: guilt isn't just a thought—it's a full-body experience.

When you rest, your nervous system doesn't just slow down. It scans for danger. If your body has learned that slowing down feels unsafe, unfamiliar, or unproductive, it will trigger internal alarms. That's not you failing. That's a dysregulated nervous system doing its job—too well.

Dr. Stephen Porges, creator of Polyvagal Theory, explains how our sense of safety isn't purely logical—it's biological. Your "social engagement system" is always looking for cues: Am I allowed to slow down? Or do I need to stay alert, perform, and keep moving to be safe?

So if you've ever felt anxious while resting? That's not proof that rest isn't for you.
That's proof that rest is something you need to relearn.

Your body needs to feel safe in rest, or it will reject it—even if your mind craves it.

The Many Faces of Rest Guilt

Rest guilt isn't just about naps and weekends. It shows up in sneaky ways:

- You multitask while "relaxing," folding laundry during a movie or answering emails during a walk.
- You feel edgy on vacation, secretly wanting to check your notifications so you don't "fall behind."
- You apologize for taking time off, over-explaining your absence, or promising to "make up for it."
- You judge others (and yourself) for "doing nothing," calling it lazy or indulgent—even when you envy it.

Rest guilt is a thief that steals your joy, your presence, and your connection to the simple pleasures of being alive.

Rest as Radical Unlearning

Here's the truth: Rest is not a reward. It is not a luxury. It is not a character flaw.
It is your birthright.

Unlearning guilt is not about bulldozing over your discomfort. It's about gently, persistently teaching your nervous system that you are safe, worthy, and allowed to stop.

It's about remembering that your value is not measured by your output; it's measured by your aliveness.

Reflection Break: Whose Voice Is the Guilt?

Take a quiet moment. Ask yourself:

1. What do I believe rest says about me?
2. Whose voice do I hear when I feel lazy, selfish, or guilty for slowing down?
3. Where did I learn that I had to earn my rest—or justify my need for it?
4. What part of me still believes that rest makes me "less than"?

Now write this (or say it aloud):

"I do not need permission to rest.
I do not need to be exhausted to deserve a break.
I am allowed to rest without explanation, justification, or apology."

Repeat it slowly. Again. And again.
Until your bones begin to believe you.

Mini Detox Practice: Guilt-Free Rest Rehearsal

Try this small but powerful act of rebellion:
For one week, schedule 15 minutes of completely unproductive rest. Call it your Guilt Rehearsal.

- No scrolling.
- No multitasking.
- No "being useful in the background."
- Just sit. Or lie down. Or stare out the window.
- Set a timer.
- Feel what comes up—and don't move to fix it.

If guilt rises, greet it. Say,
"I see you. I know you're trying to keep me safe. But I'm safe now. This is allowed."

The goal isn't to eliminate guilt immediately.
The goal is to build the capacity to rest with the guilt—and stay anyway.

Over time, your body will begin to believe the truth your brain is relearning:
Rest isn't dangerous. It's divine.

Permission to Pause

You are not selfish for resting.
You are not lazy for pausing.
You are not falling behind when you choose to be still.

You are returning.
To your breath.
To your body.
To the rhythm of being that existed long before you learned
to equate stillness with shame.

You were not made to hustle endlessly.
You were made to feel.
You were made to live.
You were made to rest—without guilt.

Let that be your quiet revolution, one breath at a time.

✦Chapter 4✦

The Nervous System of a Burnout Babe

How Chronic Doing Hijacks Your Body's Stress Response—and What to Do About It

Let's talk about your body.

Not in terms of how it looks. Not in terms of what it can accomplish, lift, tone, or hustle through. But in terms of how it responds to your life. Because while your brain is busy making to-do lists, your nervous system is quietly keeping score—long after the tasks are done.

If you're someone who runs on cortisol, thrives in chaos, or breaks out in guilt sweat the minute you sit still, this isn't about motivation or willpower. This is about survival.

Your nervous system isn't judging you. It's doing exactly what it was designed to do: keep you safe, regulated, and alive.

But here's the problem—
If you've spent most of your life equating productivity with safety, your body may have learned that rest is dangerous. And that's where burnout begins.

Understanding Your Nervous System: A Crash Course in Survival Mode

Let's pull back the curtain and look at what's happening under the hood. Your autonomic nervous system is basically the emotional weather app of your life, constantly checking for threats, opportunities, and ways to keep you alive.

There are two main modes:

- **Sympathetic (fight or flight):** Alert, focused, go-go-go. This is your "I've got this" mode, great for running from lions (or deadlines).
- **Parasympathetic (rest and digest):** Calm, soft, slow. This is the mode where your body heals, repairs, and restores.

In a healthy cycle, your body shifts between these two states fluidly. You hustle a little, then rest. You activate, then recover. Think of it like a wave—movement, pause, movement, pause. This is how we're designed: pulsing, not sprinting endlessly.

But if you've been living in chronic stress, overfunctioning, or emotional hypervigilance (constantly scanning for what's next, what's wrong, or what needs fixing), your body can get stuck in sympathetic mode. Forever on. Always wired. Never safe to slow down.

Enter: The Polyvagal Theory

Dr. Stephen Porges, the brilliant mind behind Polyvagal Theory, expands this understanding by adding another key player: the vagus nerve, your body's internal "safety monitor." When the vagus nerve perceives threat—real or emotional—it signals your body to stay on alert.

Here's the kicker: your body doesn't care if the threat is an actual tiger, a passive-aggressive email, or the memory of being ignored as a kid. Emotional threat counts too.
So if slowing down once meant getting in trouble...
If resting meant feeling invisible...
If being soft meant being unsafe...
Then your body remembers.

No matter how much you want to rest, your body is still bracing, ready for the next thing, the next demand, the next sprint.

Burnout Isn't Weakness. It's Overuse.

Burnout isn't a failure of strength. It's a failure of rhythm.

You've just been stuck in "on" mode for too long.

Your system is doing its best with what it knows. All those muscle knots, the hyper-planning, the inability to rest without multitasking—that's not brokenness. That's protection.

Your body is not betraying you. It's trying to keep you alive.

Let's get specific:

- Chronic tension in your jaw, shoulders, or gut? Your body's way of bracing for impact.
- Racing thoughts and restless legs at bedtime? Your system keeping you "ready."
- Feeling weirdly anxious on vacation or your day off? Your body isn't sure "off" is safe.

You're not lazy if you can't relax. You're not weak if rest makes you itchy.

You're just a human with a nervous system that's been trapped in hustle for too long.

But here's what your body needs to know now:

"We're not in danger anymore.
We don't have to prove our worth to feel safe.
Rest isn't abandonment.
It's home."

The Body Remembers—But It Can Relearn

Here's the beautiful part:
Your nervous system is plastic. That means it can change.
You can teach your body, with gentle repetition, that stillness
is safe. That rest is allowed. That you're not being left behind
or left out if you pause.

This doesn't happen overnight. If you've spent years, even
decades, in fight-or-flight, your system will need practice. It
will need proof. It will need patience.

Why We Get "Addicted" to Stress

Let's talk about stress hormones for a moment. When you're
in hustle mode, your brain releases adrenaline and cortisol.
These chemicals make you alert, focused, and ready to act.
But they're also addictive. You get used to the rush, the edge,
the feeling of "I'm in control because I'm moving."

When you finally stop, your body can go into a kind of withdrawal. You may feel tired, foggy, or even sad. You might crave the chaos, just to feel "normal." This is why many high-achievers sabotage their own rest—they're not used to stillness, so they create more to do.

But, friend, you are allowed to be more than a crisis manager.

Stories from the Hustle Frontlines

Consider Maya, a single parent and project manager, who once felt "lazy" if she wasn't doing three things at once. Or Alex, who only felt alive in the adrenaline of deadlines, but crashed into exhaustion every Sunday. Or Samira, who, after years of caretaking, would wake up at 3 am, mind racing, unable to remember the last time she felt truly safe.

They all had one thing in common: their nervous systems had forgotten rest was an option. But with practice, patience, and permission, even the most burned-out bodies can learn to trust stillness again.

Reflection Break: What Does Safety Feel Like?

Close your eyes. Breathe deep. Ask yourself:

1. What does my body feel like when I'm rushing? When I'm hustling? When I'm "on"?
2. What sensations arise when I try to slow down? (Restlessness? Guilt? Panic? Shame?)
3. Where do I feel safe? With whom? Doing what?
4. What tiny act helps me soften—even for a moment?

And now this:

"My body doesn't need to perform to be loved.
My rest is not a threat.
I am allowed to rewire safety around stillness."

Mini Detox Practice: The 60-Second Reset

Once a day—anywhere, anytime—try this simple nervous system reset:

Step 1: Orient.
Look around the room. Name five things you can see.
Remind your body: we're here now. We're safe.

Step 2: Exhale twice as long.
Inhale for a count of four. Exhale for a count of eight. Repeat three times. This signals your vagus nerve to calm the hell down.

Step 3: Place a hand on your chest.

Say aloud or silently:

"We don't have to earn this moment. We're allowed to be here."

This isn't just woo woo. It's neuroscience.
You're retraining your system to trust stillness again.

And that trust? That's where real restoration begins.

Permission to Come Home

You are not broken for needing rest.
You are not failing for feeling fried.
You are not lazy because your nervous system is asking for softness.

You've been surviving in sympathetic overdrive for too long.
But now?

Now you're remembering how to come home.
Not to productivity. Not to performance.

To your own peace.

Let yourself be soft.
Let yourself belong to your body again.

Let your nervous system learn that rest is not a threat—it's your birthright.

One breath, one gentle reset, one safe pause at a time.

Part II: The Anatomy of Overfunctioning

✦Chapter 5✦

Healing from Hyper-Functioning

Why You're Addicted to Being the Capable One—
and How to Stop Carrying It All

Somewhere along the line, you became the one who held it all.

You carried your responsibilities. And theirs. You held the emotions in the room. You held the plan, the schedule, the groceries, the family calendar, the team's success, the smile that kept the peace. You were the glue, the calendar, the lighthouse, the air traffic controller, and—on some days—the emotional life raft for people who never even noticed you were treading water.

And if we're being really honest?
You carried the illusion that if you didn't do it, everything might fall apart.

That's not because you're controlling.
That's not because you think you're better.
That's because, at some deep level, your body made a bargain:

"If I keep everything running, I won't be abandoned.

If I stay useful, I'll be safe.

If I do it all, no one can blame me."

Welcome to the hidden trauma response known as **hyper-functioning**.

What Is Hyper-Functioning?

Hyper-functioning is when you consistently overperform, over-give, over-commit, and override your own needs in the name of being "capable." You become the person who anticipates every need, smooths every rough edge, and catches every ball before it can hit the floor.

It often looks like:

- Never asking for help, even when you're drowning.
- Showing up as the "strong one" in every dynamic.
- Anticipating everyone's needs before your own even register.
- Feeling intense guilt if you say no—even to the smallest ask.
- Downplaying your exhaustion because "someone always has it worse."

- Fixing, mothering, managing, and mediating—often without being asked.
- Apologizing when you finally can't keep up, as if your limits are a personal failing.

It's not glamorous. It's not noble. It's not strength.
It's adaptation.

And most of the time, it starts in childhood—when being emotionally attuned, helpful, or competent became the way you received praise, avoided conflict, or kept things predictable.

You learned:
Doing keeps you safe. Needing makes you vulnerable.

So you became what the world admired: responsible, selfless, unfailing.
But inside? You're running on fumes.

Hyper-Functioning in Real Life: Stories from the Edge

Let's get tangible.

- **Nadia** volunteers for every committee at work, always brings the extra snacks, and is the first to notice when someone is having a rough day—but can't remember the last time someone asked how she was.
- **Jules** is the "rock" in their family, the one who organizes holidays, smooths over fights, and takes care of aging parents and siblings—while quietly resenting that no one ever checks on them.
- **Marcus** is the "fixer" in his friend group, the one everyone calls in a crisis, who never says no—until he crashes, burned out and angry, then feels guilty for needing space.

You see, hyper-functioning is a suit of armor. It looks like confidence and capability, but underneath, it's a patchwork of old fears:

If I'm not useful, will I be left behind?

If I don't hold it all, will everything fall apart?

If I say no, will I still be loved?

How Trauma Disguises Itself as High Achievement

Dr. Nicole LePera (aka The Holistic Psychologist) speaks often of how trauma doesn't always look like chaos. Sometimes, it looks like over-control.

- When you weren't allowed to have needs, you learned to meet everyone else's.
- When your environment felt unstable, you learned to plan for everything.
- When your worth felt conditional, you learned to outperform.

That's not ego.
That's emotional survival strategy.

The world will praise it. Bosses will reward it. Friends will rely on it. Partners will expect it.

But here's what they won't always see:
You're exhausted.
You're resentful.
You're lonely.
And you don't know how to stop.

Because here's the catch:

The more you perform as "the capable one," the less people think to check in, offer help, or even notice your fatigue. You become invisible—except for the things you do. Your needs? They get buried under the mountain of what you accomplish for others.

The Cost of Carrying It All

Let's name what it costs:

- **Your Health:** Headaches, insomnia, chronic tension, and mysterious illnesses that flare up only when you (finally) pause.
- **Your Relationships:** You may become resentful or distant, feeling like no one ever reciprocates or shows up for you.
- **Your Joy:** Life becomes a series of tasks, not moments of presence or pleasure.
- **Your Authenticity:** It's hard to let anyone see your vulnerable, messy, or needy sides. You hide behind the mask of "I've got it."

And most heartbreakingly—

Your sense of being loved for who you are, not just what you do.

Why Is It So Hard to Stop?

Hyper-functioning is sticky. Even when you're aware of it, the urge to fix, help, and overdo can be almost compulsive. Why?

- **Fear of Rejection:** If I stop carrying it, will I still belong?
- **Guilt:** What if someone else suffers because I set a boundary?
- **Shame:** Who am I if I'm not the reliable one?
- **Lack of Practice:** If you've never been cared for, asking for help feels like jumping off a cliff.

But here's the truth:
You are not abandoning anyone by putting something down.
You are coming home to yourself.

How to Start Healing

Healing from hyper-functioning is not about swinging to the other extreme and refusing to help or show up. It's about balance. It's about letting yourself be whole—a person, not a role.

It starts with tiny, brave acts of imperfection:

- Letting an email go unanswered.
- Saying "I need help" or "I can't do that right now."
- Letting someone else take the lead, even if it's messy.
- Admitting, even just to yourself, "I'm tired, and I need care."

You might be surprised: the world doesn't collapse. The people who matter will step up. And if they don't? That's data, not a judgment of your worth.

Reflection Break: Who Are You Without the Doing?

Ask yourself:

1. Who am I when I'm not being the responsible one?
2. What am I afraid will happen if I stop carrying it all?
3. Where did I learn that strength meant silence, independence, or self-sacrifice?
4. What would it look like to be loved when I'm not holding it together?

Now gently write this reminder:

"I am not only valuable when I'm strong.
I am not only lovable when I'm useful.
I do not need to carry it all to belong."

Say it again, slower each time, until it lands somewhere deeper than your to-do list.

Mini Detox Practice: Let Something Drop

Once this week—just once—let something drop.

- Don't reply to the email.
- Don't fix their problem.
- Don't volunteer for the thing.
- Don't clean it up.
- Don't offer to take it on.

Let it be imperfect. Let it fall. Let someone else step up—or let it stay undone.

Then notice:

- What does your body do?
- What stories rise up?
- What voices whisper guilt or fear?

Name them. Breathe through them. And say:

"I am not here to earn rest through performance.
I am allowed to put things down."

You may feel restless or anxious at first. That's normal. It's
your nervous system adjusting to a new truth:
You are allowed to be cared for, too.

Permission to Belong—Without Overfunctioning

You don't need to be the strong one anymore.
You don't need to be the capable one all the time.

You are not abandoning yourself by resting.
You are reintroducing yourself to the life you were meant to
live.

The one that doesn't require over-functioning to feel loved.
The one where your value is not a performance, but a
birthright.
The one where you can finally set down what was never
yours to carry—and let the world hold you, too.

Let this be your first, gentle step.

Let something drop.

And notice:

The world will keep spinning.

And you—precious, exhausted, brave you—will finally get to breathe.

✦Chapter 6✦

Stillness Is Not a Performance

How to Stop "Resting with Guilt on the Side" and Start Letting Yourself Actually Pause

You finally cleared your schedule.

You lit the candle. You poured the tea. You turned on the soft playlist or sat outside or curled up on the couch with your phone nowhere in sight. You told yourself: This is my rest time.

And yet...

Your jaw is tight. Your shoulders are still creeping toward your ears. Your mind is quietly scanning for what you should be doing next. You're resting, technically—but it doesn't feel restful. It feels... performative. Hollow. Like another task to tick off.

This, love, is the trap of performative stillness.

It's what happens when we try to do nothing—but only if we're doing it well. When rest becomes another thing to optimize. When we try to "be calm" with the same striving energy we use to conquer our inbox. We light the incense and put on the meditation app, but underneath it all, we're still bracing, still fidgeting, still half-listening for the next demand.

And while the outside world might see you resting, your inner world is still on high alert.

The question isn't: "Are you resting?"
The question is: "Is your rest actually reaching you?"

When Rest Becomes Another Costume

Let's name the ways we perform rest:

- Resting but feeling guilty the entire time ("I should be folding laundry...")
- Pausing but only so you can "be more productive later" ("I'll rest now so I can work better after lunch...")
- Meditating but judging yourself the whole time for doing it wrong ("Why can't I clear my mind? Everyone else seems to...")
- Taking time off but secretly working in the background (answering emails on vacation, "just checking in" while home sick)

- Feeling shame for slowing down and calling it "lazy" in your head

This isn't rest.
This is rest with a side of performance anxiety.

It's the nervous system still whispering, "Hurry up and relax so we can get back to earning our worth."
It's the voice that says, "You can sit, but only if you do it right. Only if you earn it. Only if you don't get too comfortable."

It's not your fault.

We live in a culture that sells "self-care" as a productivity hack. That wraps capitalism in eucalyptus oil and tells you to take a bubble bath so you can go back to the grind with a better attitude. We're taught that rest is a tool for better labor, not for deeper living.

But rest isn't about being more useful.

Rest is about reclaiming yourself.

The Roots of Performative Rest

Let's go deeper. Why is it so hard to just...stop? To sink into stillness without feeling like you're "doing it wrong"?

For many of us, the roots go all the way down to childhood and culture:

- **If you grew up in a family where busyness was prized, stillness may feel like failure.**
- **If you learned that worth is measured by achievement, "unproductive" moments feel unsafe.**
- **If you were praised for "helping out" or "being useful," then sitting down feels like a betrayal of who you're supposed to be.**
- **If you've ever been called lazy, selfish, or unmotivated just for resting, those labels echo in your mind whenever you pause.**

Over time, stillness becomes another mask to wear. Something to be good at, something to prove. Not a homecoming, but a test.

Rest Is Resistance (and Not Just a Buzzword)

Enter: Tricia Hersey, founder of The Nap Ministry and a powerful voice in the radical rest movement.

Her message?
"Rest is resistance."

Not a luxury. Not a productivity tool. Not a privilege you earn through collapse. But an act of refusal in a culture that wants your exhaustion as proof of your value.

When you choose to rest without guilt, without performance, without apology—you're reclaiming your humanity in a system that constantly tries to reduce you to your output.

That's not selfish. That's sacred.

Rest is not a loophole in capitalism. It's a refusal to play by its rules. It's a declaration: "I am more than what I produce. I am more than my usefulness. I am worthy of care, simply because I exist."

Why Real Rest Can Feel Uncomfortable

If you're used to overdoing, true stillness can feel itchy, wrong, or even scary. It's like stepping into a quiet room after years of loud noise—your senses strain, your mind searches for the old familiar chaos.

- **You might feel an urge to check your phone, fold laundry, or make a list.**
- **You might feel frustration or anxiety rise up ("I'm not doing this right!")**
- **You might hear an inner critic say, "Other people are working harder. Who do you think you are?"**

That discomfort is not a sign you're failing at rest.
It's a sign you are exiting the highway of hustle and your nervous system is adjusting to a new speed.

Reflection Break: Are You Actually Resting?

Take an honest inventory. No shame—just truth.

1. When I "rest," do I feel the need to justify it to others?
2. Do I rest only to be more productive later?
3. What does my inner voice say when I'm resting? Is it kind? Anxious? Guilt-ridden?
4. What would rest feel like if it didn't have to look any particular way?

Write your answers. Name what's true for you.

Then, read this slowly, as many times as you need:

"I am not here to perform peace.

I am here to feel it.

I am allowed to rest without an audience.

My stillness is sacred—even if no one sees it."

Let it settle in your bones.

Mini Detox Practice: Unstructured Stillness

This week, practice unstructured rest.

Here's how:

- Choose a 20–30 minute window. (Start with 5 minutes if that feels safer.)
- No goals. No apps. No timers. No outcomes.
- No journaling unless it calls you.
- No checking how "relaxed" you feel.
- Just be.

Sit. Walk. Stare at the sky. Rock in a chair. Lie down. Breathe.

Let your body find its own rhythm. Notice the world around you—the light, the sounds, the small movements.

Notice when the urge to "optimize" creeps in—and let it pass.

If you feel anxious or uncomfortable, name it. "This is the part of me that feels unsafe when I'm not performing." Breathe. Stay.

You're not trying to be "good" at resting.
You're practicing letting go of the part of you that only feels safe when you're productive.

It might feel uncomfortable. That's okay.

Stillness isn't a reward—it's a return.
A return to your body.
A return to yourself.

Permission to Be Unimpressive

You don't need to perform your pause.
You don't need to explain your stillness.
You don't need to earn your right to exist quietly, gently, fully.

You are not an algorithm.
You are not a brand.
You are not a walking checklist.

You are a living, breathing, feeling being.
And sometimes, the most rebellious thing you can do is sit down, unplug, and be absolutely, gloriously unimpressive—on purpose.

Let your rest be messy.
Let it be real.
Let it be yours—no audience, no applause, no metrics.

Because you don't have to do stillness.
You just have to let it in.

Rest is not a performance.
Rest is your birthright.
Come home to it.
Again and again.

✦Chapter 7✦

The Productivity Persona

Dismantling the Identity You Built Around Being Useful, Capable, and Always "On"

There's a version of you the world knows well.

This is the person who always responds. The one who remembers the birthday, organizes the spreadsheet, anticipates everyone's needs, shows up early, stays late, and never lets a ball drop. Impressive. Admired. Respected.

So damn capable it hurts.

And secretly? It *does* hurt.

Because while everyone else is praising the persona, you're quietly drowning inside of it. You've become the one who has it all together—but no one stops to ask if you feel together. No one offers to carry what you always seem able to hold.

And maybe... maybe you don't know how to put it down without feeling like you're disappointing everyone. Maybe the idea of letting go—of not being the one who always holds it all—feels like a risk you're not sure you know how to take.

This is the productivity persona.

It's not who you *are*.
It's who you *became*.

To feel needed.
To avoid rejection.
To survive in a world that praises function over feeling.

But you don't have to keep it anymore.

The Mask of Capability: How the Persona Was Built

This persona didn't form overnight.

It was built, brick by brick, through experiences that taught you:

- "If I don't handle it, no one will."
- "If I make a mistake, I'll be punished or rejected."
- "If I'm not helpful, I'm invisible."
- "If I'm too soft, I won't be taken seriously."

Maybe you received praise when you stepped up early.
Maybe you got attention when you were impressive, but not when you were playful, lost, or unsure. Maybe you learned to

anticipate needs because the adults around you were unreliable, distracted, or overwhelmed.

So you became capable.
Composed.
Controlled.

You traded rest for reliability.
You traded self-expression for likability.
You traded your softness for competence.

And it worked—for a while. You earned trust. You held it all. You made it look easy.

But now, you're craving something deeper.

Not just approval. Not just success.

You're craving authenticity. The feeling of being *real*—messy, soft, human, and seen.

And that means finally asking the question you've been afraid to face:

"Who am I without all this doing?"

Why the Productivity Persona Feels So Safe

Here's what neuroscience tells us: the brain loves predictability. Even if the role we're playing is exhausting, if it's predictable—it feels safe.

Our nervous system, designed for survival, will always choose the familiar over the unknown. Even if the familiar is lonely, heavy, or unsatisfying.

So, shedding the productivity persona won't feel freeing at first. It may feel destabilizing. Like you're taking off armor in a battlefield.

Because it is armor.

- It's armor against criticism.
- Armor against chaos.
- Armor against feeling left out or unseen.

But here's the twist:

That armor is heavy.
It's lonely.
It's built for protection, not connection.

And eventually, it cuts you off from your own aliveness.

You start to believe your worth is conditional. That you must *earn* every moment of tenderness by being tough, every bit of belonging by being useful. You begin to disappear inside the role you perform.

But the truth is:

- You don't need to be the one who holds it all to be loved.
- You don't need to prove your worth to be safe.
- You don't need to earn tenderness by being tough.

You can be held, too.

The Invisible Labor of the Productivity Persona

Let's be honest: carrying this persona means invisibly laboring every day, in ways most people never see.

- You keep the group chat alive.
- You remember who's gluten-free at the potluck.
- You notice the tension in the room and smooth it over before it erupts.
- You anticipate needs, solve problems before they're spoken, and clean up messes no one else even notices.

This invisible labor is exhausting. And the more capable you appear, the less likely anyone is to check if you're okay, to offer help, or to even *see* you beyond your usefulness.

You might even start resenting others for not seeing your effort, not offering to help, not realizing how much you're holding. But how could they, when your mask is so convincing?

The Cost of "Always On"

What does living inside the productivity persona actually cost?

- **Your physical health:** Chronic tension, headaches, digestive issues, fatigue.
- **Your mental space:** Racing thoughts, perfectionism, anxiety about dropping the ball.
- **Your emotional world:** Loneliness, resentment, numbness, grief for the parts of you that have to stay hidden.
- **Your sense of self:** You start to forget what you want, what you like, what rest even feels like.

You may even find yourself envying people who *aren't* so responsible. Who can be messy, needy, uncertain, or imperfect—and still be loved.

Why Letting Go Feels So Scary

Releasing the productivity persona isn't just about changing habits. It's about changing your sense of *who you are*. And that's hard.

- If you've always been the "strong one," showing softness can feel like a betrayal of your identity.
- If you've always been the "helper," asking for care can feel risky, even shameful.
- If you've always been the "organized one," letting things be messy can feel like chaos.

Your nervous system may sound the alarm. Old stories may surface: "You'll be rejected." "You'll be criticized." "You'll disappear."

But here's the radical invitation:
What if you could be loved—truly loved—without all the doing?
Who might you become if you didn't have to earn your place?

Reflection Break: Meeting the Persona

Take a few moments with your journal, your breath, your honesty.

1. **What are the traits of my productivity persona?**
   (Is this version always capable, calm, perfect, put-together? The fixer, the stabilizer, the one who never lets anyone down?)

2. **Where did I first learn I needed to become this way?**
   (Who rewarded that behavior? Who modeled it? Who needed me to be this way?)

3. **What am I afraid would happen if I stopped being this persona for a day, a week, a season?**
   (Would the world fall apart? Would I be abandoned? Would I lose my value?)

4. **What parts of my true self have I hidden in order to maintain this persona?**
   (Playfulness? Creativity? Vulnerability? Messiness? Desire?)

Now say this softly to yourself, as both gratitude and permission:

"Thank you for keeping me safe, capable one.
But I don't need to perform strength anymore.
I can be seen and still be safe.
I can be soft and still be strong."

Mini Detox Practice: Softness Rehearsal

This week, practice not being the "together" one in one small, intentional way.

Some ideas:

- Let a message go unanswered.
- Say, "I don't know."
- Let someone else take the lead—even if it's imperfect.
- Tell someone you're not okay—even if you usually are.
- Wear something cozy, messy, or comfortable instead of curated.
- Let the dishes sit in the sink, the email wait until tomorrow, the meeting run without your steady hand.

Then notice:

- **What happens inside your body?**
- **What fears surface?**
- **What relief creeps in?**

- **What new possibilities open up when you're not holding it all?**

You're not dismantling who you are.
You're just releasing the part of you that thought you had to be a superhero to be loved.

Let the mask fall, even for a moment.
Let yourself be a person—not a persona.

Permission to Unmask

You don't have to be the one who always knows.
You don't have to be the one who never drops the ball.
You don't have to keep carrying the mask of "capable" when all you really want is to be cared for, too.

You're not just allowed to rest.
You're allowed to unmask.
And you'll still be enough.

Even—especially—when you're soft, uncertain, and gloriously human.

Because the world needs more of *you*—not just what you can do.

Let yourself put down what was never yours to carry alone.

Let your softness be seen.

Let your realness breathe.

You're not alone.

You're allowed to come home to yourself.

You are not your productivity.

You are not your persona.

You are deeply, beautifully enough—just as you are.

✦Chapter 8✦

Redefining Worth Without the Résumé

How to Measure Your Value Without Metrics, Milestones, or Constant Output

For a long time, your worth was a report card.

Then it became a résumé.
A job title.
A clean kitchen.
A glowing performance review.
An inbox at zero.
A color-coded calendar.
A stack of checked-off to-dos.

It became the way people described you:

- "Always on top of things."
- "So productive."
- "A machine."

It became what you offered in every relationship:

- "I can help."
- "I'll handle it."

- "I've got this."

And somewhere along the way, you forgot:

Your value is not in what you produce.
Your value is in who you are when you're not
producing anything at all.

Why We Keep Tying Worth to Output

Let's be honest—most of us were raised in systems that
rewarded achievement and overlooked essence.

You got the praise when you performed well.
You got the attention when you excelled.
You felt safest when you were "useful."
You were most lovable when you were impressive.

So of course you built a life around doing.
You learned to earn your belonging.

And in a world where entire careers and identities are built
around metrics, milestones, and "what do you do?" small
talk—unhooking your worth from your output feels like
walking through a fog with no compass.

It's disorienting to imagine a self that isn't measured by grades, performance, or productivity. But there's a deeper question waiting beneath it all:

What if I could belong, just by being?

The Cost of a Life Measured in Output

Let's name what it costs when your value is tied to output:

- **Anxious self-monitoring.** Every moment is scored, tracked, and analyzed for worthiness.
- **Never-ending pressure.** Even after a win, the next goal is looming.
- **Fragile self-esteem.** Praise feels good, but criticism cuts deep, and silence is even worse.
- **Emptiness in stillness.** When you finally stop, you may feel lost or irrelevant.
- **Fear of falling behind.** Rest becomes a threat, not a refuge.

It's exhausting. And it's lonely—because deep down, you wonder: If I stopped performing, would I still be loved?

The Science of Self-Worth (Without External Validation)

Psychologist Kristin Neff, known for her work on self-compassion, distinguishes between self-esteem (based on evaluation) and self-worth (based on inherent value).

- **Self-esteem** says:
  "I feel good about myself because I'm doing well."
- **Self-worth** says:
  "I feel good about myself because I'm human—and that's enough."

Self-esteem fluctuates with success and failure.
Self-worth? That's the solid ground beneath it all.

But most of us have built our sense of value on conditional scaffolding:

- Approval from authority figures
- Validation from bosses, partners, or social media
- Achievement, productivity, and being useful

And when the accolades slow down, when the kids grow up, when the job changes, when the body shifts—our scaffolding shakes.

So the work now isn't to do more.

It's to remember who you are without the gold stars.

Rediscovering Your Inherent Value

What if you could remember your worth the way a child or a beloved animal does? Worthy not because of what you offer, but because you exist. Worthy whether you're sparkling or struggling. Worthy in pajamas as much as in polished attire.

This doesn't mean abandoning effort or ambition. It means unhooking your value from the metrics that will never love you back.

Imagine the freedom of living each day knowing:

- You are enough, even before you begin.
- You are lovable, even when you're not useful.
- You are worthy, even if today you rest, stumble, or simply "are."

The Challenge of Unlearning

Unlearning this old framework is not easy. The world is full of reminders to measure up. It may feel vulnerable—even rebellious—to say, "I am enough, right here, right now, with nothing to prove."

But consider:
When you meet someone you love, you don't tally their to-dos or weigh their worth by their LinkedIn profile. You love them for their laugh, their presence, their quirks and kindness.
Can you offer even a fraction of that unconditionality to yourself?

Reflection Break: Beyond the Metrics

Take a breath. Then take your journal. Ask:

1. **If I had no titles, roles, or achievements—who would I be?**
2. **Where do I feel most me, even if it's not productive or impressive?**
3. **What parts of myself do I like, even when no one's watching?**
4. **What would it feel like to measure my life in peace, not performance?**

Now whisper this into your bones:

"My value is not up for debate.
It is not a goal I reach.
It is not a reward I earn.
I was enough before I proved anything.
I will still be enough when I produce nothing."

Let it settle. Let it echo. Let it become a new foundation.

Mini Detox Practice: The Worth Inventory

Each day this week, write down one way you mattered without producing.
Big or small, visible or invisible.

It could be:

- A moment of deep listening
- Making someone laugh
- Holding space for yourself
- Letting something be messy
- Choosing gentleness over perfection
- Being present with a loved one
- Offering a smile to a stranger
- Allowing yourself to rest

At the end of the week, read your list out loud. Let your nervous system feel it. Let the non-doing, the soft power, the unquantifiable truth of who you are settle into your cells.

You are not your résumé.
You are not your productivity.
You are not your output.

You are a presence.
A soul.
A life force.

And that is plenty.

Permission to Be Enough

You were never supposed to be a machine.

You were always meant to be a miracle in motion—not because of what you do, but because of what you are:

Alive. Worthy. Here.

Even when you rest.
Even when you stop.
Even when you don't produce a single thing today.

You are still good.
Still whole.
Still sacred.

Let that truth land, again and again.
You are enough, always.

Part III: Reclaiming Rhythm, Rest, and Real Life

✦Chapter 9✦

Reclaiming Your Rhythm

Creating a Life That Honors Your Cycles—Not Capitalism's Clock

You were never meant to live in a straight line.

You were built in cycles.
You pulse. You flow. You expand and contract.
You are energy, yes—but not *constant* energy.

You were never designed to "go hard" from 8 to 6, five days a week, 50 weeks a year, with two weeks off to recover from the damage.

And yet, that's what grind culture demands.
It wants you predictable.
Efficient.
Replicable.
Resilient without ever resting.

It wants you to perform like a machine and then wonder why you feel broken when you can't keep up.

But you're not broken.
You're just out of rhythm.

And this chapter?
It's your permission slip to stop adapting to a pace that was never meant for you—and to start listening to the wisdom that lives in your body, not just your planner.

The Lie of the Linear Day

Let's get honest about where this straight-line expectation comes from.

Capitalism, industrialism, and the 40-hour work week were never designed around human wellness. They were designed around productivity and control.

The "ideal worker" is a myth:
Someone with no caregiving responsibilities, no chronic pain, no emotional dips, no creative waves—just consistent, clock-in, clock-out energy on demand.

Sound familiar?

That's not you.
That's no one.

Yet, so many of us continue to shape our lives, expectations, and sense of self-worth around that rhythm—and shame ourselves when we can't keep up.

But here's the truth:
Your energy is not linear.

- It's lunar.
- It's seasonal.
- It's hormonal.
- It's emotional.
- It's impacted by trauma, sleep, sunlight, sensory input, spiritual bandwidth—and so much more.

You're not failing.
You're overriding your natural design.

Remembering the Body's Clock

So let's talk about what real rhythm looks like—biology, not busyness:

- **Circadian rhythms** govern your sleep-wake cycle. Disrupt them, and you'll feel foggy, anxious, or wired at the wrong times.

- **Ultradian rhythms** control your energy waves within the day. Neuroscience shows your brain can only focus deeply for 90–120 minutes before needing to rest and reset—even if you ignore it.
- **Infradian rhythms** (such as menstrual cycles) impact energy, cognition, and mood across a month, not just a day. For many, these changes are profound and real.
- **Seasonal rhythms** shift your energy across the year. You're not meant to bloom 365 days a year; sometimes you're meant to rest, reflect, or quietly renew.

Rest isn't random.
It's biological.

Slowness isn't weakness.
It's synchronization.

You're not meant to hustle every day.
You're meant to tune in.

Why We Ignore Our Cycles

So why do we override all this wisdom?

- We're taught to ignore tiredness, hunger, and discomfort in favor of productivity.
- We learn to push through, to "fake it till you make it," to treat downtime like a flaw to be fixed.
- We internalize the message that only results matter and that cycles are inconvenient, maybe even shameful.

But this linear ideal is a lie.

It's a mismatch for the messy, miraculous, living system that is *you*.

When you push through fatigue, ignore pain, and force yourself into someone else's schedule, you're not building resilience—you're eroding your connection to yourself.

The Cost of Living Out of Sync

Here's what happens when you override your rhythm:

- You burn out faster, physically and emotionally.
- Your creativity dries up.
- Your immune system weakens.
- You become irritable, anxious, or numb.
- You stop trusting your own cues and needs.

And worst of all?

You miss the unique beauty of your own ebbs and flows.

Tuning In: What Does Your Rhythm Really Look Like?

It takes courage to slow down, to listen, and to trust that your cycles are not a liability but a superpower.

- Maybe you're a morning thinker and an afternoon dreamer.
- Maybe your best ideas come in bursts, not in steady streams.
- Maybe you need more rest in winter, more movement in summer, more stillness after stress.
- Maybe you need regular pauses, not just one "big" vacation a year.

Your rhythm is yours to discover and protect.

Reflection Break: What's Your Real Rhythm?

Take a quiet moment. Ask:

1. **When in the day do I naturally feel most energized, most foggy, most calm?**

2. **What part of the month or season do I feel more inward, more expressive, more still?**
3. **When am I overriding my body's cues because of guilt, pressure, or expectation?**
4. **What would my days look like if I honored energy over obligation?**

Now write this:

"I am not designed for constant output.
I am allowed to rest, pause, and follow the tides within me.
My rhythm is holy—even when it's inconvenient."

Let it be a vow. Let it be a revolt against the machine.

ini Detox Practice: Rhythm Rebuild Starter Plan

Try this for one week. Think of it as your Rhythm Recovery Ritual.

1. Track your energy in a simple way:
Morning, midday, evening. (Use ✿ for high energy, ✆ for mid, ✸ for low.)

2. Pause every 90 minutes.

Even for 5 minutes. No screens. Just breathe. Reset.

3. Build in "white space."

One daily activity that is not productive—but pleasurable. Walk, stretch, lie down, stare at the ceiling, hum a song.

4. Adjust where you can.

If you know your mornings are foggy, don't schedule your hardest tasks there. If your energy dips by 3pm, plan your rest before you crash.

5. Notice how you feel when you honor your body's signals—and how you feel when you override them.

Start designing your days around your nervous system—not just your notifications.

You are allowed to rest before you're exhausted.
You are allowed to honor your rhythm—even if the world doesn't.

Permission to Be Cyclical

You are not behind.
You are not broken.
You are just real.

You are cyclical.
You are divine.
You are alive.

And now?
You're reclaiming the rhythm that was always yours.

Let your days be wavy, not linear.
Let your needs change with the tides.
Let your rest be a revolution.

You are not a machine.
You are a living, breathing, pulsing presence.

And as you reclaim your rhythm, you reclaim your life.

✦Chapter 10✦

The Pleasure of Doing "Nothing"

Why Slowness, Savouring, and Presence Are Not Just Allowed—They're Holy

Let's reclaim a word that's been weaponized for far too long: **Nothing.**

When someone says, "I didn't do anything today," it usually comes with a shrug, a wince, or a self-deprecating laugh. As if "nothing" is failure. As if "nothing" is wasted space. As if a day without visible progress is a day that doesn't count.

But here's the truth:
Doing nothing is one of the most subversive, sacred, and soul-saving things you can do in a world obsessed with proof.

This chapter is not about laziness. It's about liberation. It's about reclaiming slowness, play, and joy—not as a side dish to your productivity, but as a main course in the feast of your life.

You are allowed to enjoy yourself.

You are allowed to linger.

You are allowed to exist in delight—not just duty.

Let's remember how.

Why We Fear Doing Nothing

Doing nothing isn't actually about inactivity. It's about being untethered to outcome. It's about unhooking your sense of value from visible achievement and letting yourself simply exist, without apology.

Doing nothing is:

- Sitting in the sun with no agenda.
- Listening to music without multitasking.
- Wandering with no goal.
- Reading for pleasure, not self-improvement.
- Resting without guilt.
- Laughing without earning it.
- Letting your thoughts drift, your body be still, your spirit simply "be."

And it terrifies us.

Why?

Because doing nothing confronts the very identity we've spent years—and sometimes a lifetime—building.

If your worth has been tied to output, doing nothing feels like erasing yourself. If your value has been performative, then "just being" feels like invisibility. If you've always been the helper, the achiever, the one who keeps it all running, then stopping can feel like losing your place in the world.

But what if that emptiness you fear is actually space? What if "nothing" is the doorway to presence, creativity, joy—and even healing?

The Radical Act of Slowness

Slowness in a world of speed is an act of rebellion.
Presence in a culture of distraction is a revolution.
Savoring life, instead of racing through it, is a return to the deepest truth of who you are.

To sit, to breathe, to notice the shifting light and the song of the birds, to let a laugh bubble up for no reason at all—these are not luxuries. They are the foundation of a life that feels like living, not just surviving.

And yet, most of us have been trained to fear "wasting time." To keep moving, keep checking, keep producing—lest we fall behind or lose our worth.

But you are not a machine.
You are not here to run an algorithm.
You are here to experience the sacredness of being alive.

Pleasure as a Form of Self-Returning

Let's talk about pleasure. Not just sensual pleasure—but soul pleasure.

- The pleasure of not rushing.
- The pleasure of laughing so hard your stomach aches.
- The pleasure of silence that feels like safety.
- The pleasure of walking barefoot through the grass, no destination in mind.
- The pleasure of sitting with a friend, or with yourself, and letting the conversation wander with no agenda.
- The pleasure of letting your mind daydream, your body rest, your spirit wander.

These moments don't look like achievement.
They don't belong in a spreadsheet.
They don't come with praise.

But they are medicine.

Neuroscience tells us that pleasure, joy, and unstructured play activate the parasympathetic nervous system—the system that signals, "You're safe now."

When you are present in your pleasure, your body begins to trust again. You begin to heal the wound of chronic urgency, perpetual "doing," and the belief that stillness is dangerous.

And for a nervous system wired for hustle, pleasure is not just allowed.
It's essential.

Healing the Wounds of "Wasted Time"

Many of us carry the wounds of shamed slowness. Maybe you were scolded for "daydreaming" or "lazing around." Maybe you were told, "Don't just sit there, do something!" Maybe your acts of joy were dismissed as silly, your moments of pause labeled as laziness.

But those moments were your first language of presence. They were the places where you met your own soul.

It's time to reclaim them.

Reflection Break: Where Does My Joy Live?

Take this slowly. Let it wake something up in you.

1. **When was the last time I did something that brought me joy with no purpose attached?**
2. **What do I love that I've labeled "unproductive"?**
3. **What did I enjoy as a child before the world convinced me to grow up and be efficient?**
4. **What does my soul crave—not for progress, but for presence?**

Now write this:

"I am allowed to do things simply because they delight me.
I am allowed to waste time beautifully.
I am not here to prove my worth. I am here to live it."

Let this be your permission slip, your gentle rebellion, your invitation home.

Mini Detox Practice: The Sacred "Nothing" Hour

Choose one hour this week and block it off.
Label it however you like:

- White space
- Soul hour
- Unstructured time
- The Great Unhustle
- Or just call it Nothing

Then... honor it.

Don't plan it. Don't perform it. Don't turn it into content. Let it be what it is: a pocket of your life where joy doesn't have to be earned and rest doesn't require explanation.

Doing nothing, when chosen with intention, becomes everything.

If discomfort arises, notice it. Breathe through it. Say to yourself, "I am safe here. I am allowed to rest. I am allowed to savor this life."

Let your nervous system relearn what it means to be at home in idle, in play, in presence.

The Sacredness of "Wasting Time"

You were not put on this earth to impress the algorithm.
You were not born to turn every moment into measurable progress.
You were not made for grind. You were made for glow.

And glow requires rest.
It requires space.
It requires the wild, rebellious act of saying:

"I am here to be, not just to do."

Time "wasted" in joy is never wasted.
Time spent delighting in your own existence is a radical act of self-worth.

Let yourself wander. Let yourself savor. Let yourself be.

You are not here for endless output.
You are here for the holy, healing, life-giving
pleasure of doing nothing at all—
and loving yourself through every unhurried,
unproductive, absolutely sacred minute.

✦Chapter 11✦

Productivity & Identity: Race, Gender, and Cultural Expectations

How different communities experience productivity pressure. Intersectional perspectives, generational cycles, and breaking the "model minority" myth.

The Myth of the Level Playing Field

Let's get honest: Productivity isn't a neutral, one-size-fits-all pressure cooker. It's a landscape shaped by culture, history, family, and the stories we inherit—sometimes without even realizing it—about what it means to be "good," "worthy," or just "enough."

If you thought hustle culture was exhausting for everyone, imagine carrying it with the added weight of racism, sexism, classism, ableism, or the immigrant dream. Sometimes, "do more" isn't just a slogan—it's a survival strategy and a family legacy. Sometimes, achievement isn't just about progress—it's about safety, legitimacy, and even love.

Let's unpack how productivity pressure gets tangled up with identity, and why unlearning it is not just a personal act, but a collective, even revolutionary, one.

When "Busy" Isn't Just About You

In the late 1980s, legal scholar Kimberlé Crenshaw coined the term "intersectionality" to describe how social identities—race, gender, class, sexuality, ability, and more—overlap and create unique forms of discrimination and pressure. While we often hear about the "universal" burnout epidemic, the truth is, the productivity hamster wheel spins at different speeds and with different stakes depending on who you are and where you come from.

Black and Brown Communities: "Twice as Hard for Half as Much"

Let's start here: For many Black and Brown folks, productivity is not just about achievement or personal fulfillment. It's about survival, safety, and fighting back against centuries-old stereotypes.

- The expectation to "work twice as hard for half as much" is not a cliché. It's a lived reality rooted in systemic barriers—from wage gaps to hiring discrimination to the criminalization of rest (think: "loitering" laws, or the way Black folks napping in public can become a police matter).

- For Black women, the "Strong Black Woman" archetype is both armor and cage: praised for resilience, but invisibilized in pain, expected to carry everyone's burdens while never showing fatigue.
- In Latinx and Indigenous communities, stories of sacrifice, collective struggle, and "making it" by working any job, any hours, are woven deeply into family lore.

Story:

Janelle, a Black engineer, remembers her grandmother's warning: "Don't ever let them see you tired." At work, she feels compelled to take on every project, mentor new hires, and always "go the extra mile"—not just for herself, but to prove that people like her belong. When she finally burned out, her boss was shocked. "But you always seemed so strong."

Gender and Femme Expectations: The Never-Ending Balancing Act

For women, femmes, and anyone expected to be a "nurturer," productivity pressure comes with an extra layer of emotional labor.

- Be accomplished, but never threatening. Nurturing, but never needy. Ambitious, but always likable. Juggle it all, smile, and don't drop a single ball.
- The "supermom" myth is relentless: parent perfectly, work tirelessly, keep the home immaculate, manage everyone's emotions, and still look "pulled together."
- For trans and nonbinary folks, there's the pressure to "prove" legitimacy through achievement, to compensate for societal bias by being exceptional, or to perform gendered expectations to stay safe.

Story:
Priya, a South Asian nonbinary artist, describes the exhaustion of trying to be "the good child" for their immigrant parents—excelling at school, supporting siblings, and never letting anyone down, all while hiding their true self. "Rest felt like a luxury I hadn't earned, and being soft felt dangerous."

Immigrants and First-Generation Folks: Hustle as Heritage

The "immigrant hustle" is often romanticized, but it's also a heavy inheritance.

- Productivity becomes a way to honor sacrifice—"My parents came here with nothing so I could have everything. How dare I rest?"
- There's pressure to fend off the myth of "laziness" or "taking advantage," to be the model minority who proves their worth through excellence.
- The "model minority" myth (especially for Asian communities) weaponizes achievement as proof of belonging—while invisibilizing pain, struggle, and the right to simply be.

Story:
Kevin, a second-generation Vietnamese American, shares: "Every time I slow down, I hear my father's voice: 'We didn't escape war for you to sleep in.' I got straight A's, a fancy job, but my body is always tense, like I'm about to be graded on how hard I'm trying."

Disability, Chronic Illness, and Capitalist Time

For disabled and chronically ill people, productivity pressure takes on a unique cruelty.

- The world expects "overcoming" or "inspiring" stories, not the truth of bodies that move at non-capitalist speeds.
- Rest is often medical, not optional—and yet, there's shame in "not pulling your weight" or "slowing others down."
- Ableist systems penalize rest: limited sick days, inaccessible workspaces, "attendance awards," and the myth that value is measured in hours worked.

Story:

Lila, who lives with lupus, describes the performance of health: "On good days, I overdo it to prove I'm 'normal.' On bad days, I hide. I don't want to be seen as unreliable, so I push until I collapse. My diagnosis gave me a reason to rest, but the guilt never left."

Generational Cycles: Inherited Hustle

Why do these pressures run so deep? Because they're generational. Maybe your grandparents survived by working sunup to sundown, your parents measured love in chores completed, and your childhood praise came fastest when you were "helpful." Generational patterns can encode hustle as both virtue and protection.

- **Survival Stories:** For many families, hard work was the difference between safety and danger, enough and not enough. Rest was a risk, not a right.
- **Shame and Sacrifice:** "Don't waste the opportunities we never had." "We didn't come this far for you to rest now."
- **Love as Labor:** If your worth was measured in what you did for others, rest can feel like rebellion—or even betrayal.

Story:

In a multigenerational home, Maya, a first-generation college student, remembers her grandmother's hands— always moving, always working. When Maya took a day to read or nap, she felt her family's disappointment like a physical weight. "Resting felt like erasing their sacrifices."

Breaking the Myth: You're More Than a Stereotype

Let's call it: The "model minority," the "strong Black woman," the "stoic immigrant," the "supermom"—these are not compliments. They're cages. They flatten humanity into performance. They erase softness, struggle, and the right to rest.

- **The model minority myth** says, "You're only as good as your achievements. Don't complain, don't struggle, don't be average."
- **The strong [insert identity] trope** says, "You don't need care. You're the caretaker."
- **The super-parent/super-worker myth** says, "Everyone's depending on you. Don't you dare let them down."

These myths are not just personally exhausting—they're socially dangerous. They uphold systems that profit from your overwork and silence your pain.

The Revolution of Refusing to Perform

What does it mean to rest in a world that has told you rest is not for you?

- **It's radical:** To nap, to pause, to say "enough," is to reject a system that measures you by your output.
- **It's collective:** When one person rests openly, it ripples out—giving permission to others. (Think of Tricia Hersey's "Nap Ministry" and the collective refusal to perform exhaustion.)
- **It's healing:** Rest is not just restoration. It's repair— of body, mind, soul, and ancestral lines.

Reflection Break: Unlearning What You Inherited

Take a breath. Then, with honesty and gentleness, ask yourself:

1. **What messages about work and worth did your family, culture, or community teach you?**
2. **When have you felt pressure to "represent," "prove them wrong," or "carry the legacy"?**
3. **How do you feel when you rest? Guilty? Anxious? Free? Invisible?**
4. **What would it feel like to rest, even if the world says you shouldn't?**

Now whisper to yourself:

"I am not a myth.
I am not a machine.
I am allowed to be human—tired, soft, real, and worthy of rest."

Mini Detox Practice: The Rest Reclamation Pledge

This week, try one act of rest that your upbringing or community might have labeled "lazy." It could be:

- Sleeping in, without apology.
- Declining an invitation to help, just because you need space.
- Letting someone else take the lead—at work, at home, in your community.
- Speaking honestly about your exhaustion, instead of performing "okay."

Notice the discomfort, the old voices, the stories that rise up. Then remind yourself: Each act of rest is a seed of healing for you and for those who come after.

Collective Wisdom: Voices from the Edges

"Rest is resistance, especially for those who were never meant to survive." —Tricia Hersey

"I am allowed to be more than what I produce, even if my ancestors could never afford that luxury." —Anonymous

- In Black feminist circles, Audre Lorde declared self-care "an act of political warfare."
- In disability justice, rest is survival: "Pacing is a radical act," says activist Leah Lakshmi Piepzna-Samarasinha.
- In immigrant communities, rest is repair: "Every nap I take is a way of saying, 'We made it. We are safe enough to rest now.'"

Moving Forward: Redefining Worth Together

So, what's next? How do you honor the stories that shaped you, but refuse to let them dictate your future?

- **Name the myths.** Write them down. Say them out loud. Let them lose their power in the light.

- **Find rest community.** Connect with others who understand the unique intersections of hustle and healing in your life.
- **Make rest visible.** Share your journey. Be the rest rebel your community needs.
- **Honor your ancestors' sacrifices—by healing what they could not.**

Final Blessing: Rest as Birthright

You are not here to be a myth.
You are not here to be a machine.
You are allowed to be human—tired, soft, real, and worthy of rest.

Your rest is a victory.
Your softness is a legacy.
Your healing is a revolution.

Rest.
Not just for you, but for everyone who ever wondered if they had to earn it.

✦Chapter 12✦

Boundaries, Burnout, and Saying No

How to set boundaries at work, in family, and with yourself. Scripts, stories, and the neuroscience of saying yes to rest.

The Most Radical Word in Self-Care

Let's talk about the dirtiest word in hustle culture: **NO**.

If you grew up on "yes," "sure," "of course," and "I'll just squeeze it in," saying no can feel like swearing in church. But here's the wild truth: boundaries aren't just about keeping things out. They're about keeping *you* in—your energy, your sanity, your sense of self.

Boundaries are the bouncers at the club of your life. They decide what—and who—gets in. Without them? You're overrun, overfunctioning, and overwhelmed, wondering why the music never stops and your feet never get off the dance floor.

Boundaries aren't about being mean. They're about being real. They're the invisible fences that make rest, joy, and authentic connection possible. And if you don't set them, someone else will—usually in ways that don't honor your needs.

Why Boundaries Are So Hard (and So Healing)

Let's get honest. Why is it so hard to say no, even when you're running on empty?

1. Fear of Disappointing Others

"If I say no, will they still love/need/choose me?"
So many of us have been taught that our worth is measured by how much we give, how available we are, how quickly we respond. The fear of letting someone down—whether a boss, a friend, or a family member—can feel like a threat to belonging.

2. Guilt

"Other people have it harder."
When your empathy is on overdrive, it's easy to convince yourself that your needs are less important. Maybe you grew up with the message that self-sacrifice is noble, and rest is indulgent. Guilt is the tax you pay for putting yourself first.

3. Habit

If you've always been the "yes" person, boundaries feel like breaking character.
Overfunctioning can become your default setting. You're so used to jumping in, helping out, and smoothing things over that you can't even remember what it feels like to pause before agreeing.

4. Hustle Brain

Rest feels unsafe; doing feels protective.
If you've survived by staying busy, boundaries can feel like dropping your guard. Doing is a shield against anxiety, uncertainty, or even old wounds. Pausing to rest can feel downright dangerous.

The Neuroscience of Boundaries (A.K.A. Why Your Brain Freaks Out)

Every time you say "yes" when you mean "no," your brain registers a micro-stress. Your limbic system (the part that handles emotions and survival) goes on high alert. If this becomes chronic, your body floods with cortisol and adrenaline. Hello, resentment, exhaustion, and eventual burnout.

On the flip side: When you set a boundary—especially one that protects your rest—your brain gets a crucial signal: "I matter. I am safe to take care of myself." Over time, this rewires your stress response and builds resilience.

Boundaries aren't selfish; they're survival.

Boundaries in Action: Real-Life Stories

At Work

Jasmine, a project manager, was the queen of "Sure, I'll take care of that." Her calendar looked like a game of Tetris. She responded to emails at midnight, took calls in the grocery store, and could recite her team's to-do list by heart. She wore her busyness like a badge—until her doctor diagnosed her with adrenal fatigue.

Her first boundary? No emails after 6 p.m. The first week, she panicked. Would the world fall apart? Would her team resent her? To her shock, nothing imploded. In fact, her colleagues started following her lead. The result? Jasmine rediscovered weekends, her creativity soared, and her body began to heal.

At Home

Dev, a parent of two, found themself trapped in the "default caregiver" role. Meals, homework, household admin, emotional support—if it had to be handled, Dev handled it. Asking for help felt like failure. But the resentment was building, and exhaustion was the soundtrack of their life.

Dev started small: "I need 30 minutes alone after dinner each night." At first, the family balked. But over time, everyone adjusted. The world didn't end. Instead, Dev returned to the dinner table more present, more patient, and more themselves.

With Yourself

Lina, a recovering perfectionist, realized their harshest boundary-breaker was...well, themself. "Just one more thing" became a mantra. Even when exhausted, they'd push through, overriding every cue from their body to rest.

Their breakthrough? Learning to notice the urge to override, and pausing. "What do I *really* need right now?" Sometimes it was a nap. Sometimes a snack. Sometimes putting the laptop away and stepping outside. The more Lina honored these micro-boundaries, the less they needed to "escape" with Netflix or sugar at the end of the day.

Scripts for Saying No (Without Apology)

Here's the truth: "No" is a complete sentence, but sometimes you want a little padding. Here are some scripts to try in real life:

- "Thank you for thinking of me, but I can't commit right now."
- "That doesn't work for me, but I hope it goes well."
- "I have to pass this time."
- "I'm at capacity, and I need to recharge."
- "I appreciate the offer, but I need to focus on my current priorities."
- "I'm practicing saying yes to rest, so I have to say no to this."
- "I need to check in with myself before I make a commitment."

Try writing your own. Practice saying them out loud. Notice what happens in your body. Sometimes just having the words ready is enough to tip you from "automatic yes" to "intentional no."

Boundaries at Work, Home, and Within

At Work

- **Protect your time blocks.** Schedule focus time—and defend it like a dragon guards gold.
- **Don't answer emails after hours.** Set an out-of-office message if you need accountability—even if you're just napping or reading.
- **Say no to "scope creep."** When your workload grows beyond your role, clarify expectations.
- **Advocate for rest-friendly policies.** Encourage breaks, flexible hours, or mental health days.

At Home

- **Share the load.** Delegate, ask for help, and let go of perfection. (Yes, the towels will be folded differently. Let it go.)
- **Block out solo time.** Even 10 minutes behind a closed door can work wonders.
- **Model boundaries for kids and partners.** Normalize rest for everyone, not just yourself.

With Yourself

- **Pause before saying yes.** "Let me check my energy and get back to you."
- **Notice when you override your own cues.** (Are you hungry, tired, overstimulated? What do you need?)
- **Set a "minimum rest" threshold.** Decide in advance how much rest you need to function—and honor it as non-negotiable.
- **Forgive yourself when you slip.** Boundaries are a practice, not a personality trait.

The Guilt Trap: Why Boundaries Make Us Squirm

Let's name it: Guilt is the shadow of every new boundary. When you're used to being the go-to, saying no can feel like you're letting everyone down. But guilt is not a reliable compass. It's just a sign that you're doing something new—something that, in time, will serve everyone better.

Remember: When you set boundaries, you're not just protecting your own well-being. You're modeling what's possible for others. You're giving your friends, family, and colleagues permission to rest, too.

Reflection Break: Your Boundaries Inventory

Take a few minutes and a piece of paper or your journal:

1. **Where do you most often override your own boundaries?** (At work? At home? With yourself?)
2. **What's the smallest "no" you can practice this week?** (It could be declining a meeting, leaving the group chat unread, or saying no to an invitation.)
3. **How does your body feel before, during, and after boundary-setting?** (Tense, anxious, relieved, proud, scared?)

Write it down. Let yourself be honest. Notice what comes up—guilt, relief, fear, freedom.

Now say to yourself:

"My rest is worth protecting.
My 'no' is a gift to my well-being."

Micro-Practices: Building Your Boundary Muscles

1. **The Pause-and-Check:** Before saying yes, take a breath and check in: "Do I *want* to do this? Do I *have* the capacity?"
2. **The "No" Challenge:** Practice saying no to something small every day for a week. Notice how your confidence grows.
3. **The Boundary Buddy:** Find a friend or colleague who's also practicing boundaries. Cheer each other on, debrief the hard moments, and celebrate the wins.
4. **The Visual Reminder:** Put a sticky note on your computer, fridge, or phone: "Rest is a boundary, too."

Advanced Boundaries: When Pushback Happens

Not everyone will love your new boundaries. Some will push back, guilt-trip, or even get angry. This is a sign your boundaries are working, not failing.

- **Expect discomfort.** It's a sign you're breaking old patterns.

- **Hold firm, kindly.** "I understand this is hard to adjust to. I care about you and I need this for my well-being."
- **Remember your why.** Boundaries make your yeses more meaningful, your relationships healthier, and your rest possible.

Final Reflection: The Ripple Effect

When you set and honor boundaries, you don't just protect your own rest—you help rewrite the culture of overfunctioning. Every "no" to hustle is a "yes" to something deeper: health, creativity, connection, and peace.

Boundaries are a gift not just to yourself but to the world. Because a rested, whole, authentic you is what we need most.

✦Chapter 13✦

Digital Detox for the Overfunctioner

How tech and an always-on world hijack our rest. Step-by-step digital detox plans, testimonies from the unplugged.

The Device in Your Hand, the Rest You Can't Find

Let's start with a confession: If your phone is the first thing you touch in the morning and the last thing you see at night, congratulations: you're human—and possibly exhausted.

You're not alone. The average American checks their phone 144 times a day. Globally, we now spend over seven hours per day looking at screens. For overfunctioners—the ones who answer emails before breakfast, scroll social media in the bathroom, and feel naked without their device—screens are both lifeline and leash.

But at what cost? In the always-on era, true rest is getting harder to find. Our brains, like our inboxes, are never empty. Our nervous systems are constantly on high alert, pinged and prodded by every notification, message, and algorithmic lure.

As rest becomes more elusive, we reach for our screens to relax—only to find ourselves even more depleted.

This chapter is for anyone who has ever tried to wind down by scrolling, only to realize it's midnight and you never even read that book you meant to start. It's for everyone who feels a tug of anxiety when their phone is out of reach, and for all those who suspect that digital overload is hijacking their rest, their focus, and, at times, their very sense of self.

The good news? With intention, support, and a little structure, you can reclaim your attention—and rediscover the deep, nourishing rest on the other side of the screen.

The Always-On Trap: How Technology Hijacks Rest

Technology is not the enemy. Our devices connect us, inform us, and sometimes even soothe us. But the design of modern tech—especially smartphones and social platforms—is not neutral. It's engineered to capture our attention, override our natural rhythms, and keep us "plugged in." Here's how:

Constant Notifications = Constant Micro-Stress

Every ping, buzz, and badge triggers a tiny burst of cortisol. These micro-stresses add up, keeping your nervous system on a low boil. Over time, this "always available" state erodes your ability to relax, focus, and sleep.

Social Media = Comparison and "Never Enough"

Scrolling through curated feeds, we compare our behind-the-scenes to everyone else's highlight reel. The result? Chronic dissatisfaction, imposter syndrome, and a nagging sense that we should be doing more, better, faster.

Work Email on Your Phone = Office in Your Pocket, 24/7

The boundary between work and rest has all but disappeared. The expectation—sometimes explicit, sometimes internalized—is that you're always reachable, always productive, always "on." True downtime feels impossible.

The Dopamine Loop

Likes, comments, new messages—these are designed to deliver tiny dopamine hits that keep you coming back, even when you don't want to. It's a behavioral slot machine, and your attention is the jackpot.

The result?

Restless sleep, fractured attention, and a sense that you can never fully "clock out." Over time, chronic digital overload leads to burnout, anxiety, and a loss of connection—to others, yes, but also to yourself.

Why Overfunctioners Are Most Vulnerable

If you're an overfunctioner, you're probably already used to being "always on." Digital life supercharges this tendency:

- **You answer work messages at all hours, "just to stay ahead."**
- **You fill every moment of downtime with productivity hacks, podcasts, or "catching up."**
- **You multitask meals, walks, even conversations—never fully unplugged.**

The result? Your brain never gets a chance to reset. The more you chase productivity through your device, the more elusive true rest becomes.

Science Break: What Screens Do to Your Brain and Body

Let's talk neurobiology. Our brains evolved for deep focus and sensory variety—walking in nature, talking face-to-face, staring at clouds. Screens, especially those engineered for engagement, hijack these ancient systems:

- **Blue light from screens** suppresses melatonin, making it harder to fall and stay asleep.
- **Endless scrolling** trains your attention span to fragment—making it harder to read, reflect, or just be.
- **Social comparison** triggers the brain's threat system, flooding you with stress hormones.
- **Information overload** exhausts your prefrontal cortex, the part of your brain responsible for decision-making and self-regulation.

The bottom line: Chronic digital stimulation leaves you wired but tired—overstimulated and undernourished, mentally and emotionally.

Step-by-Step Digital Detox for Overfunctioners

Ready to reclaim your rest? Here's a practical, compassionate plan. Remember: This isn't about perfection or puritanism. It's about small, sustainable changes that make space for rest and real life.

Step 1: Audit Your Apps

Take a hard look at your home screen. Which apps truly serve you, and which are energy vampires?

- **Action:** For one week, track your screen time and emotional state after using each app.
- **Ask:** What drains you? What inspires or nourishes you?
- **Do:** Delete, pause, or hide the apps that leave you depleted. Move nourishing ones (music, meditation, books) to the front.

Step 2: Notification Fast

Turn off all but essential notifications for 24 hours.

- **Action:** Start with social media, email, and news.

- **Result:** Notice the immediate drop in anxiety and the rise in focus.

Step 3: Tech-Free Zones

Designate spaces and times where screens are not allowed.

- **Ideas:**
  - No screens in bed (buy an alarm clock if needed).
  - No phones at meals—solo or with others.
  - No devices during nature time (walks, parks, backyard).
- **Tip:** Use a physical "parking lot" for devices during these times.

Step 4: Set an Out-of-Office (For Your Brain)

Schedule daily "airplane mode" time, even if just 20 minutes.

- **Action:** Choose a window (maybe right after work, or before bed) and commit to zero screens.
- **Bonus:** Use this time to stretch, meditate, journal, or simply do nothing.

Step 5: Replace, Don't Just Remove

Filling the digital void with analog joy is key.

- **Ideas:**
    - Read a real book or magazine.
    - Listen to music or a record (not a playlist you endlessly skip through).
    - Doodle, knit, cook, garden—use your hands.
    - Call a friend, write a letter, or daydream.

Step 6: Gradual Deepening

Once the basics feel doable, try a longer detox: a tech-free morning, a whole weekend day, or even a vacation. Plan in advance, and let loved ones know how to reach you in an emergency.

Testimonies from the Unplugged

Here's what people discover when they unplug—even briefly:

"I remembered how to daydream."
After a week without morning scrolling, I found myself staring out the window, letting my mind wander. It felt strange at first, but then ideas and memories surfaced—stuff I forgot I cared about.

"My anxiety dropped after one week of no social scroll before bed."

I started feeling less wired and more able to sleep. I didn't realize how much social media was winding me up.

"My relationships deepened when I stopped multitasking with my phone."

My partner and I started having real conversations at dinner, not just parallel scrolling. I felt more present, more connected.

Story:

Rafael, a high school teacher, realized he was living half his life through his phone. "I'd check Twitter at red lights, during staff meetings, even while playing with my kids. I tried a 24-hour digital sabbath. The first few hours were hell—restless, twitchy, like I'd lost a limb. But by the end of the day, my mind felt quieter, and I noticed the way my daughter's laugh would echo in the hallway. I got hooked on being present."

The Emotional Detox: What You'll Feel When You Unplug

Unplugging isn't just about breaking a tech habit—it's about making space for the feelings and needs that screens often mask.

- **Boredom:** At first, you'll crave stimulation. Let yourself be bored—this is where creativity and rest are born.
- **Anxiety:** You might worry about missing out, falling behind, or being unresponsive. Notice the discomfort, and remind yourself it will pass.
- **Relief:** Over time, your nervous system will downshift. You'll sleep better, think more clearly, and discover a quieter kind of joy.

Reflection Break: Your Digital Self-Inventory

Grab your journal, or just pause to consider:

1. **What's your relationship to your devices?** (Supportive, addictive, ambivalent?)
2. **What would you gain if you unplugged, even briefly?** (Peace, time, creativity, rest?)

3. **How does your mind feel after 24 screen-free hours?** (Jittery, clear, nostalgic, hopeful?)

Write down your answers. No judgment—just notice.

Micro-Practices for Digital Rest

- **Phone-Free Mornings:** Start your day with 15-30 minutes of no screens. Stretch, sip coffee, or just breathe.
- **Analog Bedtime:** Replace nighttime scrolling with a book, gentle music, or a handwritten gratitude list.
- **Tech Sabbath:** Pick one day a week (or even just a few hours) where you unplug completely.
- **Nature Breaks:** Leave your phone behind during walks or outdoor time. Let your senses recalibrate.

The Ripple Effect: What Changes When You Unplug

When you create digital boundaries, you don't just reclaim time—you reclaim selfhood.

- **Attention returns:** You can read, think, and focus more deeply.

- **Rest deepens:** Sleep improves; your nervous system finds its rhythm.
- **Relationships heal:** Presence returns to meals, conversations, and play.
- **Creativity blooms:** Boredom breeds new ideas.

Gentle Re-Entry: Using Tech Intentionally

This isn't about demonizing technology. It's about choice. When you return to your devices, choose with awareness:

- **Curate your feeds:** Unfollow accounts that drain you; follow ones that inspire, educate, or delight.
- **Batch your tasks:** Check email or social media at set times, not all day.
- **Celebrate your limits:** Boundaries are not restrictions—they're invitations to live more fully.

Final Reminder: Coming Home to Yourself

Unplugging isn't withdrawal. It's coming home to yourself. It's remembering what your own mind sounds like, what your own body feels like, what your own life tastes like— unfiltered, undistracted, and real.

"My rest is worth protecting.

My 'no' is a gift to my well-being.

When I unplug, I come home to myself."

✦Chapter 14✦

The Rest Revolution: Movements and Communities

Profiles of rest activists, "slow" movements, and what we can learn from reclaiming collective rest.

When Rest Becomes a Rallying Cry

We live in a world that treats exhaustion as a badge of honor and rest as a personal failing. But across the globe, something is shifting. Tired of burnout, disconnection, and the cult of busyness, people are gathering, organizing, and dreaming of a new way. Rest is not just a personal project—it's a movement. It's as collective as a protest, as intimate as a nap, as radical as saying, "We all deserve to stop."

This chapter is an invitation to see rest as a public good, a right, and a rebellion. We will meet the rest rebels, explore the movements that put quality over speed, and imagine how communities—large and small—can reclaim rest together.

Meet the Rest Rebels

Tricia Hersey & The Nap Ministry: Rest as Resistance

No movement for collective rest would be complete without naming Tricia Hersey, founder of The Nap Ministry. Hersey's message is simple and profound: "Rest is resistance." For her, naps are not just personal self-care—they are acts of political defiance, especially for Black people whose rest has been stolen by centuries of enslavement, exploitation, and the ongoing violence of capitalism.

The Nap Ministry organizes collective napping events, offers public education, and fills social media feeds with reminders that "you are not a machine." Hersey encourages us to see rest as reparations, as healing, as a reclamation of humanity itself. In her words:

"Rest is a form of resistance because it disrupts and pushes back against capitalism and white supremacy. We will rest!"

Story:
At a Nap Ministry event in Atlanta, dozens of strangers gather in a sunlit hall. Some settle onto yoga mats, others curl up on benches. There's no agenda except to rest

together, to be witnessed in stillness, and to remember that rest can be communal, not just individual.

Slow Food, Slow Living, Slow Cities: Choosing Quality Over Speed

Born in Italy in the 1980s as a response to fast food, the **Slow Food Movement** champions local cuisine, traditional recipes, and the joy of shared meals. But it has grown far beyond the table. Now there are **Slow Cities**— places that prioritize walkability, sustainability, and community connection. There's **Slow Living**, too: a philosophy that values depth, quality, and presence over constant acceleration.

Principles of the Slow Movement:

- Savoring rather than rushing.
- Local over global.
- Connection over convenience.
- Enough over endless more.

Story:

In the town of Bra, Italy, "slow" is a way of life. Markets are local and seasonal. Meals stretch over hours, not minutes.

Children play in town squares while grown-ups swap stories. There's time to talk, to taste, to rest.

Siesta Culture: Napping as a Collective Ritual

In Spain, Italy, Greece, and parts of Latin America and West Africa, the **siesta** is woven into daily life. Shops close, streets empty, and people retreat for a midday break. In Nigeria, the "afternoon rest" is a tradition respected across generations. In Mexico, the siesta is a legacy of pre-colonial rhythms, adapted to the midday heat.

Key lesson:
Rest is not laziness. It's wisdom—an adaptation to climate, a pause for renewal, a glue for families and communities.

Story:
Lucía, who grew up in Seville, remembers the city's hush after lunch. "The streets go quiet, shutters are drawn, and everyone disappears for an hour or two. As a child, I thought it was boring. Now as an adult, I see it as a gift."

Restorative Justice Circles: Slowing Down for Healing

In indigenous and restorative justice traditions, **healing circles** or **restorative circles** invite people to slow down, listen deeply, and repair harm together. Rest here is not just physical—it's emotional and relational. The pace is deliberate, the silences honored, the process more important than the outcome.

Key lesson:
Sometimes, the most radical thing a community can do is slow down, listen, and make space for everyone's truth.

Story:
At a restorative justice circle in Minneapolis, community members gather after a conflict. Instead of rushing to fix, they listen. There are long pauses, deep breaths, and tears. The group trusts that healing takes time—and that time is sacred.

Why Collective Rest Matters

1. It Challenges "Productivity as Worth"

When groups rest together, they push back against the idea that value is measured in output. They say, "We are more than what we produce." This is especially powerful for communities historically denied the right to rest—whether through slavery, colonization, or economic exploitation.

2. It Heals Generational Exhaustion

Communal rest interrupts generational cycles of overwork. It models for children—and for each other—that exhaustion is not inevitable, and that rest can be an inheritance, not just a reward.

3. It Offers Belonging and Permission

For those who have always had to hustle—immigrants, caregivers, activists, marginalized folks—collective rest offers something rare: permission. When rest is normalized, it becomes safer, less shameful, and more possible.

4. It Sparks Creativity and Connection

Shared rest—whether conversation, silence, or sleep—creates space for new ideas, deeper relationships, and a sense of collective possibility.

How to Join the Revolution

The rest revolution is not all or nothing. It grows through small acts, shared experiments, and everyday rituals. Here's how you can join (and lead!) the movement:

1. Start a Rest Club

Gather friends, neighbors, or colleagues for a regular rest session—no agenda except showing up and slowing down. Nap together, meditate, read, or simply sit in silence. Make rest visible and communal.

2. Host a Screen-Free Dinner

Invite loved ones for a meal with no phones, TVs, or distractions. Linger at the table. Savor each bite. Let conversation and laughter be the main course.

3. Advocate for Rest at Work

Push for workplace policies that honor rest—flexible hours, real lunch breaks, mental health days, nap rooms. Challenge the culture of overwork by modeling healthy boundaries.

4. Share Your Rest Story

Talk about your journey with rest. Post about your naps, your slow walks, your moments of stillness. The more we speak of rest, the more normal—and revolutionary—it becomes.

5. Learn from Other Cultures

Ask elders or newcomers about their traditions of rest. What rituals, rhythms, or beliefs can you adapt or honor in your own life?

6. Make Rest a Collective Priority

Organize community events around rest: outdoor yoga, quiet hours at the library, neighborhood walks. Petition for local policies that support leisure—green spaces, benches, public hammocks.

Profiles in Rest: Global Voices

- **Japan's Inemuri:** The art of "being present while napping." Inemuri is accepted—even respected—in workplaces and on public transportation. It's a sign of dedication and being part of the group.
- **Sweden's Fika:** A daily coffee break that's about more than caffeine—it's a ritual of pausing, connecting, and resting together.
- **Botswana's Go Slow Days:** In some rural areas, communities designate entire days for slowing down, reflecting, and reconnecting.

The Future of Rest: What Happens When We Slow Down Together?

Imagine a city where no one is shamed for napping in the park. Workplaces where rest is a right, not a reward. Families who gather for naps as easily as for meals. Movements that build not just on urgency, but on sustainability.

When we reclaim collective rest, we change the script of what it means to be human. We plant seeds for a world where rest is not selfish, but solidarity.

Reflection Break

1. **What would it mean for your community to truly value rest?**
   (Picture your neighborhood, workplace, or family: What changes? What feels possible?)
2. **Who in your world needs permission to rest?**
   (How can you help grant it—by modeling, inviting, or advocating?)
3. **What tradition or ritual of collective rest could you start?**
   (A rest club, a screen-free meal, a Sunday nap hour?)

Write down your answers. Dream big.

Final Affirmation: Rest Is Solidarity

Say it to yourself, your friends, your community:

"Rest is not selfish. Rest is solidarity.
My rest is a gift to myself and to the world.
When I rest, I help make rest possible for others.
Together, we can build a world where everyone gets to stop, breathe, and belong."

✦Chapter 15✦

Rest and Relationships: How Overfunctioning Impacts Intimacy

How hustle culture seeps into love, friendship, and family—and how to build connections that value presence over performance.

The Invisible Labor of "Doing" Love

Let's be real: Overfunctioning isn't just a solo gig. If you're always "doing"—planning, fixing, anticipating, handling, and smoothing over—you're probably carrying the emotional labor of every relationship you're in. You're the friend who organizes the group chat, the partner who keeps the calendar, the sibling who remembers every birthday, the parent who runs on empty just to keep the wheels turning.

But here's the truth: All that "doing" comes at a cost—one that's often invisible, cumulative, and, over time, corrosive to intimacy. Hustle culture doesn't just steal our rest. It seeps into our closest bonds, replacing presence with performance, connection with caretaking, and vulnerability with relentless competence.

What happens when we measure our worth not by who we are, but by what we give? And what does it take to build relationships that value being over doing? Let's dig in.

The Hidden Cost of Hustle Love

Overfunctioners often pride themselves on being reliable, indispensable, and perpetually available. But these superpowers can become kryptonite in our relationships—especially when exhaustion, resentment, or loneliness creep in.

Let's name the patterns:

Caretaking as Connection: Always Fixing, Never Receiving

If you've learned to equate love with caretaking, you might find yourself *doing* for others as your main love language—anticipating needs, solving problems, smoothing rough edges. It feels good (for a while) to be needed. But over time, this can tip into codependency or martyrdom, where you're always giving and never receiving.

- You offer advice before you're asked.

- You jump in to fix feelings, logistics, or even someone else's discomfort.
- You struggle to ask for help, fearing it makes you "needy" or "a burden."

Story:

Elena, a nurse and mother of three, always considered herself the "glue" of her family. She ran the household, managed everyone's schedules, and anticipated every crisis. But at night, she felt lonely—even in a full house. "No one knows what I need," she realized. "But I've never let them see me need anything."

Busyness as Avoidance: Using Tasks to Dodge Vulnerability

Sometimes "doing" is a shield against feeling. When you're busy, you don't have to get quiet enough to notice what's hurting—or to let anyone else in.

- You fill every moment with activity, even when there's nothing urgent.
- You volunteer for extra projects, chores, or errands rather than sit with hard emotions.
- You keep conversations on the surface, never quite getting to what matters.

Story:

Alex, freshly out of college, found that every time a relationship got too close, he'd become "too busy"—taking on overtime at work, planning trips, or filling weekends with friends. "If I slow down," he admitted, "I'll have to face how scared I am of being loved for who I am, not what I do."

Performing "Okay" for Others: Hiding Exhaustion, Never Asking for Help

In hustle culture, vulnerability is often seen as weakness. So you keep showing up—smiling, managing, performing "okay"—even when you're running on fumes.

- You brush off offers of help ("I'm fine!").
- You hide your tiredness, sadness, or overwhelm.
- You feel responsible for everyone else's comfort, never your own.

Story:

Marcus, a first-generation college student, felt pressure to represent his family's dreams. He worked two jobs, aced his classes, and organized campus events. "People see me as the strong one," he said. "But I'm scared to let anyone know how tired I am. What if they stop respecting me?"

Why Overfunctioners Struggle with Receiving

Many of us learned early that love means *giving*—not *receiving*. Maybe you grew up in a family where care was transactional, or where your needs took a back seat to everyone else's. Maybe you learned that being "good" meant being useful, reliable, or selfless.

But here's the paradox: True intimacy requires not just giving, but allowing yourself to be seen, held, and cared for. When you measure your worth by what you do, it's hard to let others meet you, nurture you, or see you unguarded. Over time, relationships become imbalanced—one person always pouring, the other always receiving.

Intimacy Gets Replaced by Efficiency

In overfunctioning relationships, everything can start to feel like a checklist:

- "Quality time" becomes a scheduled obligation, sandwiched between errands.
- Conversations are efficient, not deep—focused on logistics, not feelings.
- Connection is measured in shared tasks, not shared presence.

The result? Relationships feel "managed," not lived. Partners, friends, or family become coworkers in the business of life, rather than companions in the art of living.

Story:

Jenna and Tom prided themselves on being a "power couple." They ran a household like a well-oiled machine. But after a decade together, they realized they couldn't remember the last time they'd just *been* together without an agenda. "We were efficient," Jenna said, "but not connected."

Presence Over Performance: The Antidote

So what does it look like to bring rest—real rest—into relationships?

1. Trade "Quality Time" on a Checklist for Actual, Undistracted Attention

Put down the phone. Close the laptop. Turn off the TV. Presence doesn't require a fancy date night—it requires your full, unhurried attention.

- Sit together in silence.
- Go for a walk without an agenda.
- Listen, really listen, without planning your response.

2. Let Someone Else Take the Lead or Offer Comfort

If you're used to being the "doer," try letting someone else care for you—even if it's uncomfortable.

- Say yes when a friend offers to bring you soup.
- Let your partner plan the weekend.
- Allow your child to "help" you, even if it's messy.

3. Practice "Lazy Love": Being Together Without an Agenda or Goal

What if the point wasn't to accomplish, fix, or improve—but just to *be*?

- Lie on the couch together and stare at the ceiling.
- Share a meal in silence.
- Nap together, or read side by side.

Story:

Maya and Priya started a Sunday ritual called "Nothing Time." No plans, no screens, no chores. Just being together, however that looked. At first, the silence was awkward. But over time, they found themselves laughing, daydreaming, and feeling closer than ever.

Scripts for Restful Relating

Sometimes you need words to disrupt old patterns. Here are a few to try:

- "Can we just hang out and do nothing together?"
- "I need to refill my cup before I pour into us."
- "I want to be real with you, even when I'm tired."
- "I'd love to just be with you tonight—no plans needed."
- "I appreciate when you take the lead sometimes. It helps me rest."
- "I'm learning to let myself be cared for, too."

Practice saying these out loud. Notice what comes up—discomfort, relief, fear, longing. That's okay. Presence grows with practice.

How Rest Deepens All Kinds of Relationships

In Romantic Partnerships

- Rest fosters vulnerability: When you're not performing, you can bring your authentic self—flaws, fatigue, and all.

- It disrupts gendered scripts: In many cultures, women are expected to do more emotional labor. Rest invites equity and mutual care.
- It sparks intimacy: Stillness allows room for affection, playful touch, and unhurried conversation.

In Friendships

- Restful friendships aren't about constant activity, but about safe space. Friends who can sit together in silence, cancel plans without guilt, or show up "as is" are gold.
- Rest lets you see—and be seen—beyond your achievements.

In Families

- Modeling rest teaches children that love isn't earned through doing. It's a birthright.
- Families that value downtime together—no agenda, just presence—build trust and resilience.

The Practice: Building Restful Bonds

1. Schedule Unstructured Time Together

Block out time for "nothing"—no chores, no projects, no screens. Let the day unfold.

2. Make Space for All Feelings

Dare to show up tired, sad, or "not okay." Let others comfort you. Practice receiving.

3. Rotate Roles

In relationships, overfunctioners often take on the same roles: planner, fixer, cheerleader. Switch it up. Let others lead, decide, or support.

4. Communicate Needs Early and Often

Don't wait until you're burnt out to ask for help. Share your needs, your limits, and your desire for rest—before you hit empty.

5. Cultivate "Presence Practices"

- Eye contact without distraction.
- Shared breathing or meditation.

- Simple touch—a hug, hand-holding, a gentle squeeze.

Reflection Break: Your Rest and Relationships Inventory

Take a moment to reflect:

1. **Where does overfunctioning show up in your relationships?**
    - Are you always the planner, the fixer, the giver?
2. **How do you feel when someone else cares for you?**
    - Relieved, awkward, unworthy, grateful?
3. **What does true presence feel like in connection?**
    - Safe, warm, vulnerable, peaceful?
4. **What's one way you can invite more rest into your relationships this week?**

Write down what you notice. Share your insights with someone you trust. Let yourself be seen.

Affirmation: Rest Is Love

Repeat to yourself, and maybe to those you love:

"My relationships thrive when I bring my whole, rested self—
not just my doing.
I am worthy of care, presence, and love—just as I am."

Closing: The Gift of Being, Together

Rest is not a withdrawal from relationship—it's a way of
being more fully present with those you love. When you stop
"doing" long enough to be seen, to receive, to simply exist
together, you invite connection that's deeper, richer, and
more sustaining than any to-do list.

The revolution begins at home, in friendship circles, in every
place you dare to rest and let yourself be loved, not for what
you do, but for who you are.

✦Chapter 16✦

Relearning Play: The Antidote to Grind

The science and soul of play for adults. Creativity, hobbies, and joyful rebellion as essential forms of rest.

The Lost Language of Play

Remember play? Not the competitive kind, but the rolling-in-the-grass, belly-laugh, lose-track-of-time kind? The kind where you forgot to worry about what others thought, where you made up your own rules, and where the only point was to enjoy being alive?

Somewhere along the winding path to adulthood, many of us lost touch with play. We traded it for productivity, for seriousness, for the belief that fun was something you earned only after the work was done. Yet, deep inside, the longing to play—to be spontaneous, curious, and creatively free—never really left.

You weren't born just to work and worry. You were made to play. And in a world that glorifies the grind, relearning play may be one of the most radical, restorative acts you can choose.

Why Do Adults Forget How to Play?

As children, play is our default mode. We explore, invent, and delight in the world around us. But as we grow, the messages change:

- "Stop fooling around."
- "Act your age."
- "Get serious about your future."

Work becomes sacred, and play is dismissed as frivolous. Many of us internalize the idea that play is for children, or at best, a guilty pleasure.

Yet, study after study shows that play is not a luxury—it's a necessity.

The Neuroscience of Play

Dr. Stuart Brown, founder of the National Institute for Play, spent decades researching the role of play in human development. His findings? Play is as essential as sleep or nutrition. Mammals deprived of play become anxious, rigid, and socially awkward. In humans, the absence of play leads to burnout, depression, and a shrinking sense of possibility.

Play as Stress Regulation

Play isn't just fun—it's a powerful regulator for our nervous system. Laughter, movement, imaginative engagement, and even light-hearted banter release tension and reduce stress hormones like cortisol. Play strengthens our capacity to adapt, recover, and heal.

Creativity and Emotional Processing

When we play, we enter a state of "flow"—that magical zone where time disappears, self-consciousness fades, and we're fully absorbed. In flow, creativity and learning skyrocket. Play also helps us process emotions: through games, art, music, and movement, we make sense of our inner world and build resilience against life's challenges.

Play Builds Connection

Shared play is social glue. It breaks down barriers, deepens relationships, and creates memories. Whether it's a board game, a jam session, or silly jokes, play reminds us that we belong.

The Science of Joy: What Play Does for Your Body and Mind

Research shows that play:

- **Reduces cortisol and other stress hormones.**
- **Releases endorphins, boosting mood and relieving pain.**
- **Increases neuroplasticity, improving learning and memory.**
- **Strengthens the immune system.**
- **Improves emotional regulation and social skills.**

Dr. Brené Brown, in her research on wholehearted living, found that adults who prioritize play are more joyful, resilient, and content. They are better able to handle stress and recover from setbacks.

Case Study:

When a Fortune 500 company introduced weekly "play breaks"—from improv games to LEGO challenges—employee satisfaction and creativity soared, while workplace stress plummeted. The most popular event? A "bring your pet to Zoom" day, filled with laughter and spontaneous connection.

Play Is Not Frivolous—It's Foundational

In a culture addicted to productivity, play is often seen as optional. But history, anthropology, and neuroscience all agree: Play is a cornerstone of human development, creativity, and well-being.

- **In indigenous societies**, play is woven into rituals, storytelling, and daily life—not as a distraction from work, but as a source of wisdom and connection.
- **In high-performing athletes and artists**, playful exploration is the secret sauce behind breakthroughs and innovation.
- **In therapy**, play is used to heal trauma, build trust, and foster growth at every age.

To play is to remember our wholeness.

How to Reclaim Play

Ready to bring play back into your life? Here's how to start— no perfection or performance required.

Try Something Silly

Start small. Choose something that makes you smile, even if it feels awkward at first.

- Dance in your kitchen to your favorite song.
- Doodle on a napkin while you sip your coffee.
- Build a pillow fort or a blanket tent—invite a friend or your inner child.
- Try on silly hats or costumes, just for a laugh.
- Make funny voices or invent a character.

Tip: When you notice self-consciousness or "this is silly" thoughts, remind yourself: Play is how I reclaim my joy.

Say Yes to Hobbies with No Outcome

Pick up a hobby that isn't about achievement, progress, or productivity.

- Paint, knit, or garden with no goal but enjoyment.
- Learn an instrument just to make noise.
- Bake something new—let it flop, and laugh about it.
- Try origami, whittling, or model trains.

Remember: The point isn't to win or improve—it's to savor the experience.

Invite Others to Play

Play is contagious. Invite friends, family, or coworkers to join you.

- Host a game night (board games, charades, trivia).
- Organize a sing-along or karaoke hour.
- Plan a "joy walk"—spotting shapes in the clouds, jumping in puddles, or inventing stories about passing strangers.
- Try a group craft, a scavenger hunt, or group storytelling.

Story:
Jorge, a retired engineer, started a weekly "play club" for neighbors of all ages. They rotated activities: sidewalk chalk, story circles, kite flying, and even a "bad joke contest." Over time, the club became the highlight of the week—and friendships deepened in ways no formal gathering could match.

Barriers to Play (and How to Move Through Them)

"I Don't Have Time"

Play doesn't require hours—just intention. Start with 5-10 minutes. Even a short burst can reset your mood and energy.

"I'm Not Creative"

Play isn't about talent. It's about curiosity. Try something new, borrow a kid's game, or let yourself be a beginner.

"I Feel Silly"

That's the point! Play invites us to drop our guard. The more you practice, the more natural it becomes.

"Play Is for Kids"

Who decided that? Research shows adults need play even more. It's how we counteract stress, monotony, and burnout.

Building Pockets of Play Into Your Routine

- **Start your day with play:** Five minutes of dancing, sketching, or singing in the shower.

- **Add play to breaks:** Try a quick doodle, a funny video, or a round of "would you rather?" with a colleague.
- **Create "play triggers":** Place a yo-yo, puzzle, or ball where you'll see it. Let it remind you to pause and play.
- **Play with pets or children:** Let them lead. Their creativity is contagious.
- **End your day playfully:** Share a joke, watch a comedy, or build a bedtime fort.

Joyful Rebellion: Why Play Is a Radical Act

Choosing play in a world obsessed with grind is an act of joyful rebellion. It's a declaration that your life is more than tasks, achievements, or worries. Play says: "I am alive. I am free. I am worthy of delight."

Movements that Center Play:

- **Cultural festivals:** From Holi in India to Carnival in Brazil, collective play brings communities together.
- **Laughter yoga:** Groups around the world gather to laugh—not because something's funny, but because laughter itself is healing.

- **Adult recess:** Companies, co-ops, and communities are bringing back recess—proving there's no age limit on joy.

Reflection Break

1. **When did you last play, just for yourself?**
   (What did it feel like? What memories does it bring up?)
2. **What playful activity calls to you now?**
   (Trust the first idea, no matter how small or silly.)
3. **How can you build pockets of play into your routine?**
   (What would make it easy, inviting, and fun?)

Jot down your answers, or share them with a friend. Let yourself dream.

Declaration: Play as Your Birthright

Say it out loud, say it to yourself, say it to your inner child:

"Play returns me to my truest, most alive self.
I am not here just to work and worry.
I am here to play, to laugh, to create, to rest.
My joy is revolutionary—and it starts with play."

The Playful Path to Rest

As you move forward, remember: Play is not a reward for grinding hard enough. It's the foundation of a life well-lived, a nervous system soothed, and a spirit set free. Every time you choose play, you rebel against the myth that adulthood must be joyless. You invite rest, creativity, and connection back into your days.

The world needs your playfulness. Start small, start now, and let yourself be surprised by joy.

✦Chapter 17✦

When the World Won't Slow Down: Rest as Rebellion

How to rest in a culture that won't let you. Strategies for "resting in public," micro-rests, and finding peace in unsupportive environments.

Daring to Rest in a Restless World

Let's be honest: the world isn't going to hand you permission to rest. In fact, it's more likely to hand you another deadline, another notification, another reason to keep moving. You might hear the message—loud and clear—that rest is for the lazy, the privileged, or the weak. That to truly belong, you must be busy. That to be worthy, you must be exhausted.

But here's the radical truth: In a society addicted to hustle, **rest is rebellion**.

This chapter is for everyone who's ever been side-eyed for taking a break, shamed for "wasting time," or told that slowing down is selfish. It's for all those who are tired of being tired—and ready to reclaim rest as a courageous, communal act.

Rest as Resistance: Why Rest Changes Everything

Rest may seem small—just a nap, a pause, a breath. But in a world that rewards burnout, every act of rest is an act of resistance. It's a refusal to let your worth be measured by your output. It's a declaration that you are not a machine. It's a reclaiming of time, space, and softness.

Resting "In Public"

When you rest openly—closing your eyes at your desk, taking a walk during lunch, saying "no" to overtime—you disrupt the status quo. You send a signal: Rest is normal. Rest is necessary. Rest is powerful.

Story:

Aisha, a bank teller, started taking her lunch breaks outside, sitting on a bench under a tree. At first, colleagues teased her: "Come back in, you'll fall behind!" But over time, a few joined her for a few minutes each day. Soon, the "bench break" became a quiet ritual, a tiny oasis in the middle of a busy city street.

The Ripple Effect

When you rest, you give others permission to do the same. You challenge the culture of hustle, one pause at a time. You remind everyone watching—including yourself—that rest is a right, not a reward.

The Backlash: When Rest Makes Others Uncomfortable

Let's face it: Not everyone will cheer for your rest revolution. Some will roll their eyes at your nap, side-eye your "slow morning," or act like rest is an indulgence. You may encounter:

- **Guilt-tripping:** "Must be nice to have time to relax."
- **Suspicion:** "Aren't you busy enough?"
- **Shaming:** "Some people don't have the luxury of rest."

It's tempting to shrink, to justify, to slip back into busyness just to fit in. But every act of rest you claim is a seed of change. It chips away at the myth that burnout is noble.

Micro-Rests for the Relentless: Finding Rest in Small Doses

What if you truly can't take a long break? What if your environment is unsupportive—or even hostile—to rest? Here's the good news: **Micro-rests matter**. Even 30 seconds of intentional pause can reset your nervous system.

1. Breath Breaks

- Between meetings, emails, or errands, take 5 slow, deep breaths.
- Inhale for 4 counts, hold for 4, exhale for 6.
- Imagine each breath as a mini "reset."

2. Two-Minute Tune-In

- Close your eyes (if you can), and listen deeply—notice the sounds around you.
- Let your attention drift from your to-do list to the present moment.
- Can't close your eyes? Just soften your gaze and tune in anyway.

3. Sunlight Pause

- Step outside, or stand by a window if that's all you have.
- Feel sunlight or fresh air on your skin for a minute or two.
- Stretch, yawn, or simply notice your surroundings.

4. The Slow Move

- Walk slowly—intentionally—between spaces.
- Let your body move at half-speed, even if just for a few steps.
- Savor the sensation of moving without rushing.

5. The Desk Drop

- Drop your shoulders, unclench your jaw, let your hands rest.
- Take a few seconds to notice tension, and release it.

Story:

Omar, a busy ER nurse, started a practice of closing his eyes for 30 seconds between patients. "I can't change the pace of the hospital, but I can change the pace inside my own body," he says. "Those tiny pauses keep me human."

Finding Peace in Unsupportive Environments

Some spaces are simply not built for rest. Maybe your workplace glorifies overtime. Maybe your family sees rest as slacking. Maybe your community values constant productivity. Here's how to anchor yourself in rest, even when the world pushes back.

Anchor Yourself: Rituals and Reminders

- Carry a calming object: a smooth stone, a worry bead, a photo, or a quote.
- Repeat a mantra: "I am allowed to rest." "I am not a machine."
- Create a mini ritual: a cup of tea, a song, a stretch— something that signals "pause" to your body and mind.

Build Rest Alliances

- Find just one "rest rebel" friend—a colleague, neighbor, or online buddy—who gets it.
- Check in with each other; share victories and setbacks.
- Normalize talking about rest, exhaustion, and boundaries.

Story:

Priya, an attorney, formed a "rest pact" with a friend in the same law firm. Each day, they texted a check-in: "Have you taken a break yet?" Knowing someone else was also resisting the grind made all the difference.

Invisible Rest: Resting When You Can't Pause Physically

- Practice gentle self-talk: "I'm doing my best. It's okay to slow down inside."
- Focus your attention on your breath, heartbeat, or a mantra.
- Shift your posture—relax your shoulders, uncross your legs, soften your hands.
- Visualize a peaceful place, even for a few seconds.

Rest as Rebellion: The Courage to Be Different

Claiming rest in a world that won't slow down is an act of hope, courage, and kindness. You won't always be understood. But every nap, every pause, every refusal to glorify exhaustion plants a seed for a different way.

Public Acts of Rest: Inspiration Across Cultures

- **Japan's Inemuri:** Sleeping in public is accepted as a sign of dedication and belonging.
- **The Nap Ministry:** Tricia Hersey and others host public rest events, inviting people to nap together as resistance.
- **Protest and Pause:** At climate strikes, disability justice rallies, and mental health marches, activists are normalizing rest tents, quiet zones, and collective breathing.

Reflection Break

1. **Where do you need to rebel against busyness?**
   (Work, family, community, inner expectations?)
2. **What tiny acts of rest can you claim, even in chaos?**
   (A breath, a pause, a "no," a moment of softness?)
3. **Who can you invite to rest with you?**
   (A friend, a coworker, a child, a stranger on the same journey?)

Write down your answers—or whisper them to yourself as a commitment.

Affirmation: Every Act of Rest Is a Seed of Change

Repeat it. Believe it. Share it.

"Every act of rest is a seed of change.
I am allowed to slow down, even when the world won't.
My rest is an act of rebellion—and an invitation to others."

Resting Forward

The world may not slow down. But you can. You can claim your right to pause, to breathe, to be. And with every micro-rest, every courageous nap, every refusal to hustle beyond your limits, you help build a world where rest is not the exception, but the expectation.

Rest is your revolution. Start wherever you are, and let the seeds you plant—with every act of rest—grow into something softer, kinder, and more human for us all.

✦Chapter 18✦

The Healing Power of Ritual and Ceremony

How intentional rituals (morning, evening, communal, seasonal) can rewire your relationship to rest and worth.

The Lost Magic of Everyday Ritual

Rituals aren't just for temples or yoga studios. They're woven into the fabric of every human society—ancient and modern, sacred and secular. Yet, in a culture obsessed with speed and efficiency, we often overlook the quiet power of ritual to soothe, ground, and restore us.

Ritual is the scaffolding of a life that honors rest, meaning, and return. It's a way of telling your body and spirit: "It's safe to slow down now. You don't have to earn this pause. Rest is your birthright."

Whether it's a morning mug of tea in the sun, a candlelit evening wind-down, or a seasonal ceremony that marks the changing tides of your year, ritual helps you claim pockets of peace—amidst chaos and noise.

In this chapter, we'll explore why rituals matter, how to create your own, and how communal and seasonal ceremonies can reconnect you to yourself and the rhythms of the living world.

Why Rituals Matter

1. They Signal Safety to Body and Mind

Rituals act as cues to your nervous system. You step into a familiar sequence—stretch, breathe, sip, listen—and your whole being receives the message: It's safe to let go. No need to stay on high alert. Rest is welcome here.

2. They Create Containers for Rest

Unlike the endless to-do list, rituals are finite and intentional. They provide a beginning and end, so you don't have to negotiate with guilt or wonder if you've "earned it." The ritual itself is the reason, the permission, and the gift.

3. They Can Be Simple or Elaborate, Solo or Shared

You don't need incense or a ceremonial robe (unless you want them!). Rituals thrive on meaning, not complexity. You can practice alone, with a partner, in a family, or with a circle of friends or neighbors. What matters is the intention you bring.

4. They Help Rewire Your Relationship to Worth

When you make rest a ritual, you retrain your mind: "My worth is not in my output, but in my being. I am allowed to pause, to savor, to belong to this moment."

Ideas for Rest Rituals

Let's get practical. Here are ways to build restorative rituals into the rhythm of your days, weeks, and seasons.

Morning Rituals

- **Stretch in Sunlight:** Before checking your phone, greet the day with gentle movement in a patch of morning light. Feel your body wake up with gratitude.
- **Sip Tea in Silence:** Choose a mug you love. Savor the warmth, the aroma, the pause.
- **Set an Intention:** Write a word or phrase for the day—"ease," "joy," "enough."

Evening Rituals

- **Gentle Music or Candlelight:** Transition from busy day to restful night with soft music or the glow of a candle.
- **Gratitude Journaling:** List three things you're thankful for, no matter how small.
- **Screen-Free Wind Down:** Replace scrolling with a comforting book, a bath, or mindful breathing.

Communal Rituals

- **Family Meal:** Make at least one meal a day or week a sacred gathering—phones away, conversation encouraged, presence prioritized.
- **Group Meditation or Quiet Time:** Whether in person or online, share silence, breath, or gentle movement.
- **Shared Walks:** Roam your neighborhood or a nearby park together, speaking or not, simply being side by side.

Seasonal Rituals

- **Mark the Equinox or Solstice:** Light a candle, gather with loved ones, or write down hopes for the new season.
- **First Snow or First Blossom:** Celebrate with pajamas and cocoa, or a picnic in the garden.
- **Harvest or Letting Go:** In autumn, release what you no longer need—old habits, clutter, resentments.

Making Rituals Your Own

- **Choose Comfort Over Performance:** If it feels forced, it's not your ritual. Pay attention to what soothes and delights you.
- **Infuse the Senses:** Use scents (lavender, cinnamon, fresh air), sounds (bells, birdsong, favorite songs), and textures (soft blankets, warm mugs) to anchor your ritual in the body.
- **Let Rituals Evolve:** Life changes—so can your rituals. What worked in one season may shift in another. Let your practices grow with you.

Story:

Ava, an overwhelmed grad student, started lighting a candle each night before bed. Sometimes she'd sit in silence, sometimes she'd journal, sometimes she'd cry. The ritual itself became her anchor—a way to signal "the day is done, and I am safe to rest."

The Communal Power of Ceremony

Rituals are even more potent when shared. Group ceremonies—potlucks, song circles, moon gatherings, or grief rituals—remind us that rest and renewal are meant to be collective.

Story:
Once a month, a group of neighbors in Minneapolis gather for a "rest potluck." Everyone brings a dish, a story, and a simple ritual—a poem, a song, a moment of silence. The evening ends with everyone lying on the floor, eyes closed, listening to music. "For two hours, we let the world wait," says one participant. "And we remember we're not alone."

Reflection Break

- **What rituals (past or present) remind you to rest?**
  (Think: family traditions, childhood routines, spiritual practices, or your own inventions.)

- **Where can you add a small ceremony of pause in your day?**
  (Is there a natural transition—waking, eating, arriving home, bedtime?)
- **How does your mind and body respond to ritualized rest?**
  (Do you feel safer, softer, more whole?)

Write your answers, or simply let yourself notice. Let ritual be a portal to peace.

Ritual as Portal

Let ritual be your invitation—a gentle bell that calls you back to yourself, again and again.

"My rituals are portals to peace,
inviting me back to myself,
one sacred pause at a time."

✦Chapter 19✦

Relapse, Repair, and Returning to Yourself

What to do when you slip back into old habits. Self-forgiveness, gentle restarts, and building a sustainable rest practice.

The Myth of the Perfect Rest Journey

Let's be honest: The rest revolution isn't a straight path. You will fall back into overdoing. You will forget, get swept up, say yes when you mean no. Congratulations—you're alive.

We are wired for habit, and hustle culture is sticky. Relapse—returning to old patterns of busyness, self-neglect, or overfunctioning—is not failure. It's part of the process. Just as in any healing practice, what matters is not avoiding all slips, but learning how to repair and return—again and again.

Why We Relapse

1. Stressful Seasons

When life ramps up—deadlines, illness, family crises—rest is often the first thing to go. We revert to survival mode, powered by adrenaline and old scripts.

2. Old Patterns, Old Voices

Many of us carry deep-seated beliefs: "Rest is lazy." "There's too much to do." "I can't let anyone down." These voices grow louder under pressure.

3. Cultural Headwinds

We're swimming upstream in a world that rewards busyness and shames slowness. Even with the best intentions, it's hard to resist the current.

4. Fear of Missing Out or Falling Behind

The anxiety that everyone else is doing more, faster, better can make rest feel risky. What if resting means being left out, losing ground, or disappointing someone?

Repair Over Perfection

The antidote to relapse isn't more willpower or self-criticism. It's repair—gentle, honest, and self-compassionate.

Notice the Slip—Without Shame

Instead of beating yourself up, get curious. What pulled you back into hustle? What were you feeling, needing, or fearing? Notice the pattern, but don't make it your identity.

Forgive Yourself

You're not performing for anyone. You're practicing—learning new rhythms, unlearning old ones. Self-forgiveness is the soil where new habits grow.

Restart Gently

Begin again, right where you are. You don't need to overhaul your life or "make up" for lost time. Try one breath, one pause, one boundary. Let it be enough.

Story:

Jorge, a teacher, noticed he was working late every night again. "I caught myself," he says, "not to punish, but to remember why I started this journey. I took a deep breath, closed the laptop, and made tea. That was my restart."

Sustainable Rest Practices

Build in Micro-Moments

If a full day off seems impossible, start with a minute of breathing, a mindful walk, or a cup of tea. Micro-rests add up and retrain your nervous system to expect gentleness.

Revisit Your Rituals

When you're off track, return to the rituals that ground you— a candle, a song, a morning stretch. Rituals make rest accessible, even when you feel lost.

Ask for Help

Rest is easier in community. Tell someone you trust that you're struggling. Invite them to rest with you, or simply to hold you accountable for slowing down.

The Gift of Returning

Every time you return to rest, you reinforce a new story: "I am worthy of care, even when I forget. My value is not in my consistency, but in my willingness to begin again."

Healing is not linear. Each return is a holy homecoming—a chance to remember, reconnect, and start anew.

Reflection Break

- **What triggers your return to hustle?**
  (Stress, comparison, loneliness, old voices?)
- **What helps you come back to rest?**
  (A friend, a ritual, a reminder, a moment of nature?)
- **How can you make repair part of your rhythm?**
  (What would it look like to normalize slip-ups and returns?)

Write your answers or reflect quietly. Let each return be gentle, not punitive.

Closing: Worthy of Rest, Always

Offer yourself this:

"I am worthy of rest, even when I forget.

Every return is a holy homecoming.

I am allowed to begin again, as many times as I need."

Part IV: Reclaiming Rhythm, Rest, and Real Life

✦Chapter 20✦

Real-Life Stories: Rest Rebels Who Changed Their Lives

You're not alone in this. Meet the everyday rest revolutionaries—teachers, parents, artists, nurses, activists, and office workers—who got tired of being tired and chose a different way.

The Power of Witnessing Change

Rest can feel lonely in a world that idolizes exhaustion. But you're not alone. All around you, ordinary people are quietly—or loudly—rebelling against grind culture. Their journeys are not perfect, but they are real, messy, and deeply inspiring.

The stories in this chapter prove that rest isn't just a theory. It's a lived revolution, possible for anyone—no matter your background, profession, or history.

Jordan: From Super-Employee to Sunday Unplugged

Jordan spent years as the go-to person at work. Emails at midnight, never-ending projects, always "on." Burnout hit hard—insomnia, chest pain, panic attacks. Desperate for change, Jordan made a radical decision: no screens or work on Sundays.

At first, the withdrawal was intense. "I felt like I was missing out, falling behind." But soon, Sundays became sacred. Jordan discovered old hobbies, new friendships, and a creative spark that had long been buried. Productivity at work improved, but more importantly, Jordan found peace and a sense of self-worth beyond output.

Alex: The Napping Club Catalyst

In college, Alex was known as the "overachiever." Between classes, internships, and student government, exhaustion was constant. After reading about The Nap Ministry, Alex started a napping club on campus—just a quiet room, mats, and a "no judgment" policy.

It quickly became the most popular group. Students napped, socialized, and shared stories of burnout. The club sparked conversations about mental health, collective care, and the right to rest. "We realized rest is contagious. When one person slows down, others follow."

Samira: Saying No to Hustle, Yes to Family

Samira, a corporate manager and mother of two, was the master of multitasking. But her health and relationships suffered. She began practicing saying "no" at work—no to late meetings, no to weekend emails. At first, anxiety spiked. But as Samira reclaimed her evenings for family dinners, laughter, and rest, everything changed.

Her kids noticed. "You're more fun now, Mom." Her marriage deepened. Even her work improved, as she became more focused and less frazzled. "Rest gave me back my life," Samira says.

Luis: Spreading the Rest Revolution Online

Luis, a digital content creator, realized that his online hustle was burning him out. He began sharing his rest journey— honest posts about naps, screen-free weekends, and the struggle to slow down. To his surprise, hundreds of followers reached out, grateful for the permission to rest.

Luis started hosting monthly "digital detox" challenges and shared resources on sustainable rest. His community grew into a movement, proving that vulnerability and authenticity can shift culture, one story at a time.

Mei: Leading "Slow Walks" for Community Healing

After a period of grief and burnout, Mei began taking slow, mindful walks in the park. She invited neighbors—young and old—to join. These monthly "slow walks" became a cherished ritual. People shared stories, noticed birds and blossoms, and found healing in nature and each other.

Mei's walks inspired others to start their own rituals—potluck dinners, poetry circles, communal naps. "We learned that slowing down is more powerful together," Mei says.

The Common Threads: Setbacks, Doubts, and Imperfect Beginnings

None of these journeys were smooth. Each rest rebel faced setbacks: relapses into overwork, skepticism from others, internalized guilt. But they kept returning—again and again—to the promise of rest.

What united them? Courage to begin. Willingness to be imperfect. And a belief that life is richer, kinder, and more connected on the other side of exhaustion.

Reflection Break

- Which story resonates most with you?
- What would your own "rest revolution" story look like?
- Who in your life might need to hear that rest is possible?

Consider sharing your own journey—with a friend, online, or in a journal. Your story may be the seed of someone else's rest.

The Invitation

The rest revolution is waiting for you. Start small. Start messy. But start. You are not alone—and your rest is a gift, both to yourself and to the world.

Final Blessing

For the One Who Thought They Had to Earn Their Worth

May you remember what your body knew before the world taught you to forget:
That your breath is enough.
That your being is enough.
That your presence—not your productivity—is your most radiant offering.

May you unhook your value from checklists, inboxes, and gold stars.
May you retire from performing "fine" when you're quietly unraveling.
May you give up the exhausting game of keeping it all together.

You were never meant to live on empty.
You were never meant to prove your usefulness with your burnout.
You were never meant to schedule your self-worth between meetings.

You were made to rest.
To pulse with seasons.
To be cyclical, tender, wild, and beautifully inefficient.

May you find freedom in slowness.
May you remember that joy is not a distraction from your life—it is your life.

May you trust that the version of you who's not constantly fixing, producing, achieving, or performing... is still deeply, wildly worthy of love.

You are not lazy.
You are healing.
You are not behind.
You are recalibrating.
You are not failing.
You are finally waking up.

So take the nap.
Skip the chore.
Say no.
Recline.
Turn off your phone.
Lose the plot.

Be gloriously, unapologetically unavailable for anything that treats your humanity as a liability.

You do not have to earn your exhale.
You do not have to justify your joy.
You are enough now.
You were always enough.
And rest is your return.

Bonus Section

Journal Prompts for the Recovering Overfunctioner

Because the hustle lives in your nervous system, not your calendar—and self-reflection is where detox begins.

1. What belief do I still carry about rest that keeps me stuck in guilt?
2. When did I learn that being productive made me more lovable?
3. What does my body feel like when I override its need for rest?
4. What part of me is still afraid to be seen *not doing*?
5. What's one thing I do only to prove I'm "enough"— and what would happen if I stopped?
6. Who benefits when I burn out? Who suffers?
7. What does "a life that feels like mine" actually look like?

Write without performing. Write without editing. Write like you're reclaiming space inside your own bones.

Rest Rebellion Ritual: A Practice for Letting Go

Burn the Checklist. Bless the Pause.

You'll need:

- A journal or loose paper
- A candle, match, or symbolic flame
- A quiet space where you won't be interrupted

Step 1: Write

On the paper, write down every unspoken rule you've lived by that has tied your worth to productivity.
Things like:

- "I must always be available."
- "If I'm not busy, I'm failing."
- "I have to prove I'm doing enough."
- "Rest is for after I've earned it."

Step 2: Burn or release

Light the candle. Read each line aloud. As you do, say:

"This is no longer my truth."
If it's safe, burn the paper (or tear it into pieces and throw it

away). As you do, breathe in the words:

"I am worthy—even when I rest."

Step 3: Replace the rules with blessings

Write 3 new truths. Blessings for your life moving forward.

- "My rest is sacred."
- "I am allowed to stop."
- "My being is more valuable than my doing."

Keep those close.

Mantras for Unhooking from Hustle

When guilt rises, when doubt creeps in, when the urge to "earn" your right to exist resurfaces—say these aloud, as often as needed.

"I rest without guilt. I pause without apology."

"My value is not measured in output."

"I am not behind. I am human."

"I am allowed to enjoy without justifying."

"Rest is not a reward—it is a right."

"Doing less doesn't make me less."

"My nervous system deserves peace, not performance."

"I can be soft. I can be still. I will still be loved."

"Unplugging is not quitting—it's remembering."
"I am not a machine. I am a miracle."

Say them until they feel like home.

Bibliography

Sources of Wisdom, Science, and Soul for a Rest-Hungry World

1. **Maté, Gabor.** *When the Body Says No: The Cost of Hidden Stress.* Vintage Canada, 2003.
   — Referenced for understanding how hyper-functioning and productivity addiction are often trauma responses rooted in early emotional survival.

2. **Neff, Kristin.** *Self-Compassion: The Proven Power of Being Kind to Yourself.* William Morrow, 2011.
   — Cited throughout for the shift from self-esteem (based on doing) to unconditional self-worth.

3. **Hersey, Tricia.** *Rest Is Resistance: A Manifesto.* Little, Brown Spark, 2022.
   — A foundational influence on reclaiming rest as a sacred act of rebellion, particularly against capitalist grind culture.

4. **Porges, Stephen W.** *The Pocket Guide to the Polyvagal Theory: The Transformative Power of Feeling Safe.* W. W. Norton & Company, 2017.
   — For understanding the vagus nerve, nervous system regulation, and the body's response to perceived safety and stillness.

5. **LePera, Nicole.** *How to Do the Work: Recognize Your Patterns, Heal from Your Past, and Create Your Self.* Harper Wave, 2021.

— Referenced for insight into the emotional patterns and protective identities we create around overachievement.

6. **Dalton-Smith, Saundra.** *Sacred Rest: Recover Your Life, Renew Your Energy, Restore Your Sanity.* FaithWords, 2017.

— Referenced for her model of the seven types of rest and the importance of holistic recovery beyond sleep.

7. **Newport, Cal.** *Deep Work: Rules for Focused Success in a Distracted World.* Grand Central Publishing, 2016.

— For historical and psychological insight into the value of rest for focus and attention—and the myths around constant productivity.

8. **Pang, Alex Soojung-Kim.** *Rest: Why You Get More Done When You Work Less.* Basic Books, 2016.

— For evidence that productivity actually increases with intentional rest, and for dismantling myths around long hours and burnout.

9. **Brown, Brené.** *The Gifts of Imperfection.* Hazelden Publishing, 2010.

— Cited for dismantling perfectionism, shame, and the performance trap that often masquerades as ambition.

10. **Hooks, bell.** *All About Love: New Visions.* William Morrow Paperbacks, 2000.
— For a reframe of love as presence, not performance—and rest as part of loving ourselves radically.

11. **Tolle, Eckhart.** *The Power of Now: A Guide to Spiritual Enlightenment.* New World Library, 1999.
— Referenced for the idea that presence—not productivity—is the highest expression of our being.

12. **Crenshaw, Kimberlé.** "Mapping the Margins: Intersectionality, Identity Politics, and Violence against Women of Color." *Stanford Law Review*, vol. 43, no. 6, 1991, pp. 1241-1299.
— For the foundational concept of intersectionality, referenced in discussions of race, gender, and productivity.

13. **Brown, Stuart.** *Play: How It Shapes the Brain, Opens the Imagination, and Invigorates the Soul.* Avery, 2010.
— For the neuroscience and essential role of play in adult well-being and creativity.

14. **Turkle, Sherry.** *Reclaiming Conversation: The Power of Talk in a Digital Age*. Penguin Press, 2015.
— For insights on digital overload, the impact of screens on intimacy and rest, and reclaiming analog connection.

15. **Odell, Jenny.** *How to Do Nothing: Resisting the Attention Economy*. Melville House, 2019.
— For the philosophy and practice of digital detox, mindfulness, and reclaiming attention.

16. **Leah Lakshmi Piepzna-Samarasinha.** *Care Work: Dreaming Disability Justice*. Arsenal Pulp Press, 2018.
— Referenced for the intersection of rest, disability justice, and collective care.

17. **Honoré, Carl.** *In Praise of Slow: Challenging the Cult of Speed*. HarperOne, 2004.
— For the history and philosophy of the Slow Movement, including slow food, slow cities, and slow living.

18. **Baldwin, James.** *The Fire Next Time*. Vintage, 1993.
— For context on generational exhaustion and the lived experience of rest as resistance in marginalized communities.

19. **Lorde, Audre.** *A Burst of Light: Essays.* Firebrand Books, 1988.

    — For the framing of self-care and rest as acts of political warfare, particularly in Black feminist and activist contexts.

20. **Kabat-Zinn, Jon.** *Wherever You Go, There You Are: Mindfulness Meditation in Everyday Life.* Hyperion, 1994.

    — For mindfulness-based approaches to rest, ritual, and the nervous system.

21. **Siegel, Daniel J.** *The Mindful Brain: Reflection and Attunement in the Cultivation of Well-Being.* W. W. Norton & Company, 2007.

    — For the science of mindfulness, attunement, and emotional regulation through rest and ritual.

22. **Social Psychology and Trauma Research (various).**

    — Including work on burnout, internalized capitalism, survival stress, and chronic over-functioning as emotional adaptation.

23. **Restorative Justice Practices (various).**

    — For understanding the power of communal slowing, restorative circles, and repair as communal rest.

24. **The Nap Ministry.** (www.thenapministry.com)

— For inspiration and practical examples of rest as collective activism.